Praise for *The Responsible Entrepreneur*

"*The Responsible Entrepreneur* is an inspiring book that tells us how to be the kind of entrepreneur that the world needs today. Carol Sanford tells vivid, compelling stories of what it means to be a successful businessperson and at the same time fundamentally change the world for the better. If every entrepreneur, aspiring entrepreneur, and entrepreneurship educator read this book, the world couldn't help but be a better place!"

> —**Pamela Hinds,** associate professor, Department of Management Science and Engineering, Stanford University

"Several decades ago, Peter Drucker declared that we were entering the Entrepreneurial Society. Carol Sanford's book *The Responsible Entrepreneur* spells out in concrete terms what it will take to make that a life-enhancing reality with responsible entrepreneurs who, instead of working *within* the system or even *despite* the system, *transform* industries and society itself."

> —**Stephen Denning,** author, *The Leader's Guide to Radical Management,* and contributor, *Forbes*

"Entrepreneurship is a way of thinking about opportunities. Carol Sanford offers frameworks to improve this thinking process based on different situations, making it possible for you, the entrepreneur, to be more creative and focused and do what you know in your gut to be right. *The Responsible Entrepreneur* makes clear that you're in charge of the vision for your venture."

> —**Connie Bourassa-Shaw,** director, Buerk Center for Entrepreneurship, Michael G. Foster Business School, University of Washington

"Businesses are arising all over the world that are designed as solutions to the biggest problems we face as human beings. *The Responsible Entrepreneur* looks deeply at these game-changing entrepreneurs and finds a pattern. Carol Sanford provides a systemic approach to intervention based on the concept of regeneration. It is worth spending time with *The Responsible Entrepreneur* and reflecting on it again and again."

> —**Kevin Jones,** cofounder, SoCap

"Being an entrepreneur is a challenge in any field. Trying to change the world through your business is an even more demanding one. Carol Sanford has given us an instruction manual that is clear and documented with case studies of people who have taken on the impossible and succeeded. You will be inspired to action and raise the level of contribution you see possible for you and your business."

—**Elliot Hoffman,** founder and CEO, Just Desserts, and
founder and CEO, True Market Solutions

"*The Responsible Entrepreneur* is one of those books that shifts the conversation. Carol Sanford provides entrepreneurs with a clearly articulated, eminently applicable framework for thought and action that will help them create businesses that—in the words of Steve Jobs—'put a dent in the universe.' If you want to build a business that will make the world a better place, *The Responsible Entrepreneur* should be your guidebook."

—**Erika Anderson,** founder and partner, Proteus,
and author, *Leading So People Will Follow*

"Entrepreneurs seeking meaningful impact need tools to be successful in their quest. *The Responsible Entrepreneur* is a necessary handbook for changemakers on the journey to use their businesses to shape a future that is healthier and more satisfying for everyone."

—**KoAnn Skrzyniarz,** founder and CEO, Sustainable Brands

"By viewing leaders through archetypal lenses, Carol provides helpful tools for categorization without limiting the unique strengths of any individual entrepreneur. *The Responsible Entrepreneur* is not for the well intentioned but for those who believe the problems we face demand better, more thoughtful, more scalable, and ultimately more human companies that create remarkable value for every stakeholder."

—**Brian Howe,** founder and CEO, Impact Hub Seattle;
founder, Vox Legal; and entrepreneur-in-residence,
University of Washington

"While each of us aspires to make a dent, most of us work where dreams and innovations are crushed. With *The Responsible Entrepreneur,* you can change all that and not just build a better widget or a better company, but a better world."

—**Nilofer Merchant,** author, *11 Rules for Creating Value in the Social Era*

"Carol Sanford introduced us to regenerative business design three decades ago—building a business based on living systems thinking that gives us systemic health. Now she tells entrepreneurs how to be big game-changers in the world of responsible entrepreneurship with disruptive transformation of industries that all businesses can achieve—making the world a better place in the process."

—**Hunter Lovins**, president, Natural Capitalism Solutions, and professor, sustainable management, Bainbridge Graduate Institute

"Responsible entrepreneurs are a rare but growing breed. The difficult challenge is staying true to our values and having the tenacity to stick with it. Thank you, Carol Sanford! Your book provides me with a great roadmap to continue moving forward with others who share our passion and vision."

—**Barbara Kimmel,** executive director, Trust Across America, Trust Around the World

"Carol Sanford's totally original, powerful framework will push entrepreneurs to ask questions that matter—and in turn, inspire them to unleash their full potential."

—**P. J. Simmons,** cofounder and chair, Corporate Eco Forum

"Carol Sanford has produced a profound but simple framework for understanding and unleashing entrepreneurial talent. Offering unique insight into four types of entrepreneurship and the domains in which they provide the most leverage, *The Responsible Entrepreneur* will feed the entrepreneurial spirit and catalyze it toward more meaningful impact in the world."

—**Lara Lee,** SVP, customer experience design, Lowe's Home Improvement, and former VP, Harley-Davidson

"In this era of growing disparity between the very rich and the rest of us, Carol Sanford provides a visionary yet practical path for how four iconic kinds of responsible entrepreneurs can be the creators of opportunity and a rising tide to lift more boats. Her explicit call for a transformation framework inspires me to play a role in this needed change. You, too, will be moved to participate and make your life's work more meaningful."

—**Kare Anderson, c**olumnist, *Forbes*, and author,
   Moving From Me to We

"Carol Sanford is as much a systems changer as the entrepreneurs she illustrates. *The Responsible Entrepreneur* offers a rational and highly accessible framework to cultivate self-awareness, entrepreneurial spirit, and the agency needed to bring about a systemic shift. By grounding her theories in story and practical application, this book is not only valuable but enjoyable."

—**Matthew Abrams,** vision keeper, Mycelium

"Carol Sanford understands the importance and the urgency of embedding a social compass into your business from the first napkin sketch. More important, she shows you how to do it. If you want to look back at your business five to ten years from now and say 'we did this the right way,' *The Responsible Entrepreneur* is your bible."

—**John Bradberry,** author, *6 Secrets to Startup Success*

"*The Responsible Entrepreneur* is packed with insight. Like Jane Jacobs, Carol Sanford offers observations from real life about how successful businesses and organizations actually work, without gloss, hype, or baloney. She brings a much bigger picture to enterprise."

—**Spencer B. Beebe,** chairman, Ecotrust

The Responsible Entrepreneur

Four Game-Changing Archetypes
for Founders, Leaders,
and Impact Investors

Carol Sanford

Foreword by John Fullerton

JB JOSSEY-BASS™

A Wiley Brand

Published by Jossey-Bass
A Wiley Brand
One Montgomery Street, Suite 1200, San Francisco, CA 94104-4594—www.josseybass.com

Jossey-Bass books and products are available through most bookstores. To contact Jossey-Bass directly call our Customer Care Department within the U.S. at 800-956-7739, outside the U.S. at 317-572-3986, or fax 317-572-4002.

Wiley publishes in a variety of print and electronic formats and by print-on-demand. Some material included with standard print versions of this book may not be included in e-books or in print-on-demand. If this book refers to media such as a CD or DVD that is not included in the version you purchased, you may download this material at http://booksupport.wiley.com. For more information about Wiley products, visit www.wiley.com.

Library of Congress Cataloging-in-Publication Data

Sanford, Carol, 1942-
  The responsible entrepreneur : four game-changing archetypes for founders, leaders, and impact investors / Carol Sanford. -- First edition.
    pages cm
  Includes bibliographical references and index.
  ISBN 978-1-118-91075-7 (hardback); ISBN 978-1-118-91072-6 (pdf); ISBN 978-1-118-91071-9 (epub)
    1. Social entrepreneurship.   2. Social responsibility of business.   I. Title.
HD60.S2493   2014
658.4'21—dc23

2014011874

Printed in the United States of America
FIRST EDITION
HB Printing   10 9 8 7 6 5 4 3 2 1

I dedicate this book to:

Noble Murray, my grandfather and keeper of our Mohawk heritage

Lois Murray Faith, my mother, who carried forward and recorded our Mohawk ancestors' stories

Maxwell Noble Packer, my grandson, a storyteller and author even at age fourteen

Sylvia Packer, my adopted granddaughter, with her own Native American and Maya heritage

Contents

Contents

Contents

Foreword

The book in your hands is a gift.

It is a gift to those who wake up in the morning and want to change the world. It is a gift to entrepreneurs seeking to pursue their highest calling. It is a gift to a new breed of investors, "impact investors," who are looking to back entrepreneurs with a social and or environmental mission, and to align their capital with their values in the process. Mostly, it is a gift to civilization, for I believe that the innovative and creative potential of entrepreneurialism, empowered by our innate goodness and unique human agency to impact the world, holds the promise of a prosperous future for our grandchildren.

It is increasingly clear to most thinking people that the first half of the twenty-first century is and will continue to be a time of great transition. Many interconnected crises—social, cultural, economic, financial, political, and ecological—are all converging at the same time, making this time one of great uncertainty fraught with profound risks. The leading institutions of the world—established in a different time, in a context no longer relevant, and for different challenges—seem hopelessly inadequate to the task at hand. While it has become a cliché among forward-thinking business leaders, it is nevertheless true that "business as usual"—returning to what worked prior to the turn of the century—is not an option. What kind of world will emerge is yet to be determined.

Yet many of our leaders from the political sphere as well as the business sphere seem largely stuck debating old twentieth-century narratives. Free markets versus regulation. Capitalism versus socialism. Conservatives versus liberals. In its more extreme form in the United States, the Tea Party versus Occupy Wall Street. If we listen to only the mainstream media and cable channels preoccupied with the fight du jour, which sells ads, we can seem hopelessly stuck.

Don't be fooled. Below the surface, profound change is afoot. Our global economy is proving its dynamism despite the extreme and destabilizing volatility resulting from these interconnected crises. That dynamism, further enabled by accelerating technological change, has bolstered the power of human agency like never before. Our human successes and failings are amplified in the process. Long-established industries, from media and entertainment to energy and manufacturing, and the nature of work itself are undergoing profound transition. So too is geopolitics, driven by the power of individual human agency—and not all of it for the better. Our mainstream "leaders" are left reacting to events they can't anticipate and don't control.

The human agency explored in this book, manifesting in what we call "entrepreneurship," is exemplified as much by Mother Teresa as it is by Steve Jobs. Individuals, acting on deeply held beliefs and passion, are boldly imagining and bringing into existence a different world. This book is about their story and our story. Drawing on archetypes from Carol's own Native American wisdom traditions, which we can all relate to, it helps us understand how this agency works, across different spheres of society, and at different levels of our economic and social systems. It helps us identify ourselves in this unfolding collective story, empowering our unique genius for greater impact. In the process, we will find greater personal fulfillment, meaning, and joy.

Carol's book is a gift, coming at this critical time, because it embodies much-needed wisdom. I have found Carol's wisdom profoundly important in my own work and feel privileged to have a direct and ongoing channel into it. Such wisdom is seldom heard in our loud and often shallow public discourse. She has a genius for framing and illuminating accessible wisdom, crystallizing for us some of the most hopeful and empowering transformations happening as a result of human agency. Suddenly, clarity and hope displace confusion and helplessness.

Several years ago, a young man named Zilong Wang wandered into my life. He had grown up in Inner Mongolia, found his way to the United States, and graduated from Hampshire College in 2013. His senior thesis was "Entrepreneurship Through Time: Genealogy and Dialectics." In his research, he found that the word "entrepreneur" is derived from the thirteenth century French verb *entreprendre*, "to undertake," and is generally associated with the world of business. Zilong also found that at least one line of thinking traces the root of the French *entreprendre* all the way back to the Sanskrit *antha prema*, sounding similar, which translates as "self-motivated."

If the Sanskrit is indeed the original root, it suggests that entrepreneurship is an innate human quality in all of us, applying to all domains of human activity. Thus our modern use of the term "social entrepreneur" carries an unnecessary modifier. The Sanskrit definition is certainly in alignment with Carol's belief in the human agency in all of us to be self-motivated—to make a contribution to something important, something meaningful. It is my hope and my conviction that, with the help and guidance of Carol's wisdom, our innate entrepreneurialism and looming events will conspire to foster the transcendence of our seemingly intractable problems. Like the end of apartheid or the demolition of the Berlin Wall—both so hard-fought for so long, yet seeming so precipitous and cathartic when they came about—such emergence has always defined the evolutionary process in nature. Why not human social and economic systems, for are we not part of nature?

Whether you're a business entrepreneur, a social entrepreneur, an investment entrepreneur, or an academic, artistic, or civil servant entrepreneur, devour this important and wise book. Harness the untapped potential of your human agency to tackle the urgent, at times daunting, yet exciting challenges we face. This is our collective twenty-first-century calling, and for me, a source of hope and great inspiration.

Thank you, Carol, for this gift.

John Fullerton
Founder and president, Capital Institute

Introduction
Our World Is Calling for a New Kind of Entrepreneur

Great companies start because the founders want to change the world . . . not make a fast buck.

—GUY KAWASAKI

Transitions can be agonizing. In recent years, the Western world has found itself at the intersection of multiple major transitions:

- Between generations, when young and old try to make sense of each other's worlds and mostly fail
- Between economic cycles, when polarized classes and political parties blame one another and exalt themselves
- Between eras, as when Rust Belt industries have given way to ubiquitous information and the death of privacy

As challenging as they may seem on the face of it, these transitions also create an edge—and a crucible where small interventions and intelligent choices can bring about big transformations. Within this crucible, the responsible entrepreneur moves behind problems and issues to work on underlying patterns. Raising understanding of how to leverage this work to create global change is the purpose of this book.

We are at a time in history when our planet is under siege, communities are filing bankruptcy, and the disparity between rich and poor has widened. From a global perspective, business has been a key contributor to this list of ills. It consumes vast resources, drives the flow of capital, and exerts a high degree of control over labor markets and conditions. Yet for these very reasons, business—especially entrepreneurial business—could just as readily be the instrument for making the world a healthier and more equitable place. That's why the world needs entrepreneurs who will push against boundaries, challenge sacred cows, and question authority and the status quo in general. In other words, we need entrepreneurs who work the edge to change the game.

The good news is there are an astounding number of people trying to figure out how to make a better world through the way they live their lives and earn their livelihoods. Universities report an explosion in the numbers of students entering business programs that focus on social change. The stage is set for a revolution in consciousness, but that revolution can't succeed if it depends on the methods that created the problems in the first place. We need advanced methodologies that are consistent with the more humane world being sought by so many at this time.

A Method to Manage the Madness

For four decades, working in very large multinational corporations and small entrepreneurial enterprises, I was able to codevelop and test such an advanced methodology. I call it *responsible business development*. At DuPont, a change effort that I helped design led to a revolutionary new way of mining and processing titanium (and associated proprietary technologies) that generated 1,000 percent growth in the business while radically reducing destructive ecological and community impacts. In South Africa in the early 1990s, I collaborated with a team from Colgate Palmolive to help the company successfully transition into a post-apartheid world by using its presence in the country to grow leadership in black townships (while also enjoying a 40 percent growth in revenues). At Seventh Generation, I cocreated a shift in company focus from philanthropy and "doing good" to moving the entire household products industry toward sustainable practices. (These, and a host of other stories, are told in depth in my book *The Responsible Business*.)

Ironically, most of the businesspeople I have collaborated with started out being "bad" with regard to one or more criteria of social or ecological responsibility. Few, if any, were interested in becoming "good." They just wanted to be better at being in business. Nevertheless, whenever I engaged them in thinking more systemically about their value-adding processes, their work became increasingly beneficial with regard to the environment and society as a whole—not through philanthropy but as a direct result of business activities.

As powerful as responsible business development has proven to be, I am clear that using it to work one business at a time is too slow. I want as many people as possible to have access to this methodology. I have a strong sense of urgency about the need for profound and rapid change—in the world in general and in business in particular. The key to this change is to cultivate in people everywhere the personal agency to pursue their desire to make a difference so that they, too, can contribute to a society that is healthier for everyone. That's what this book is for.

Primary Characteristics of the New Entrepreneur

I am a big fan of entrepreneurs and the entrepreneurial spirit. At its best, entrepreneurialism combines initiative, innovation, and risk-taking with a desire to bring real value to the world. To do this requires tenaciously challenging the limits (perceived or real) of what is possible. When that tenacity yields a breakthrough, the effect can ripple out far beyond the reach of any individual business.

Responsible entrepreneurs are a special breed. They start out with the idea of changing the game of business itself, to make business a force for making the world a better place. They have the courage to take on what they don't yet know how to do and the dedication to build the capability to do it. These entrepreneurs are driven by the realization that society and the planet need something big from them and that, if they don't rise to the challenge, the work may not get done.

Reimagining the World of Entrepreneurship

After years of teaching and studying how systemic change happens, I have been able to organize and make sense of what I have observed by drawing from something my grandfather, Noble Murray, taught me. His heritage and upbringing were Mohawk, and he believed that a healthy tribe could emerge and sustain itself only when four major archetypes—the Warrior, the Clown, the Hunter, and the Headman—were present and working collaboratively. Each archetype informed a unique kind of leadership, and each was necessary for the well-being of the community. I have used these archetypes to illuminate four key frames of reference that are common to all of the entrepreneurial agents of change whom I have encountered.

Leveraging Entrepreneurship to Accelerate Change

It is easy to confuse responsible entrepreneurs with those who wish to make their businesses role models. Good role-model businesses strive to be exemplars of social or environmental responsibility. They seek to do the right thing and thereby inspire others to emulate them. As worthy as this endeavor is, it is not what I am describing here.

Responsible entrepreneurs seek to actually transform industries and society itself. They challenge and refine cultural assumptions, laws, regulations, and even the processes of governance. But this requires them to enlarge their perspectives and their capacities far beyond what is usually required of business leaders. That is, they need to reimagine their *role* in business and society in order to raise themselves to a level where they can negotiate the internal and external challenges that will inevitably arise at this level of transformational game. The four archetypes featured in this book are intended to serve as guides and aids for anyone stepping up this new, more demanding way of doing business.

I have directed this book toward entrepreneurs because I believe that they are the ones with the will to work in a sustained way on innovation and transformation. Because healthy economies are critical to bringing about change, the business entrepreneur plays a highly leveraged role. I feel it is increasingly important to engage with entrepreneurs, because I observe that far too many of them violate their own values by heedlessly adopting outdated corporate ideas, believing that they have no other choice if they are to succeed. Still others believe that they need to leave business and take on social advocacy if they are to bring about important changes. These entrepreneurs clearly recognize the power of business to be a destructive force, but they seem to forget that this same power could be used for life-affirming transformation.

This book is also directed toward impact investors, who play a critical role in fostering health-generating businesses. Responsible investors also seek a method to generate new insight into where to invest, how to measure results, and how to advise investees. Too often, the change models offered to investors draw on old thinking and outgrown paradigms. *The Responsible Entrepreneur* proposes an alternative, systemic approach. I believe that impact investors can greatly leverage the change efforts they support through the use of the leadership archetypes presented here.

Entrepreneurship Is Everyone's Birthright

Not everyone becomes a global change agent, but I believe that anyone of us can, if we strive to. From my perspective, too many people are blind to their own potential and the difference they could make. "Don't think small," I want to tell them. "There's so much to do. We need every one of us to help if we're going to change all of the games that are at play right now—games that diminish potential for families, communities, nations, and Earth. We must know ourselves to be powerful and self-determining, able to respond to the call for a healthier and more vital society. Even the smallest business has an opportunity to contribute to this important work.

This book is dedicated to the entrepreneurial spirit, wherever it is found. It makes no difference whether you are an entrepreneur in your own company or within a large organization. If you are an impact investor who thinks like an entrepreneur, you can use the frameworks offered here to evaluate and direct your investments to create the greatest benefit to all stakeholders. Entrepreneurialism is a perspective or worldview that can be practiced anywhere.

Responsible Entrepreneurs Rise Above Rugged Individualism

Entrepreneurialism is about personal agency and the development of will. I'm particularly interested in the growth and expression of *will* in creative enterprise. This is why entrepreneurship matters, because human will is a powerful and necessary social force if we are to successfully undertake major change on a global scale.

The idea of the entrepreneur is almost worshipped in the United States. It reflects one of the qualities that make the country unique—a tendency toward rugged individualism. It is associated with the ideas of innovation, creativity, and a willingness to take great risks in pursuit of a dream. The word *entrepreneur* comes from the French and means *an enterprising individual who builds value through initiative or by taking risks*. In ordinary conversation, the word is also used to describe a person who launches something new and accepts full responsibility for the outcome.

Around the United States and the world, an exciting upwelling of entrepreneurial spirit seems to be taking place in local and community endeavors, as people who never thought of themselves as entrepreneurs are inspired to take on the role.[1] For example, enthusiasts of local foods are birthing businesses in major cities everywhere, and young people are experimenting with new forms and definitions of business. Meanwhile, crowd-funding has made a big dent in the backlog of startup funding needs; in 2012, it raised over half the capital available on the planet.[2] Even recent high unemployment has turned out to have a silver lining, stimulating a host of new start-ups. The next generation of entrepreneurs is at this very moment inventing new products, industries, sources of capital, and models of enterprise. In the process they are creating the necessary proving ground, as well as the competence and confidence, for the emergence of the responsible entrepreneur as a business paradigm for the twenty-first century.

Latent Entrepreneurship Identifiers

The entrepreneurial spirit is a core human trait that shows up wherever personal agency and will are present. Entrepreneurs can be found in all walks of life. Some work for themselves, others work in large organizations, but all of them share certain characteristics:

- They care about the whole of something and enjoy developing the acumen needed to work on all parts of a business. Even with regard to those aspects that don't thrill them, they are tenacious about doing what it takes to get something launched.
- They maintain their own motivation, getting stimulus, training, and information when they need it. They work hard to manage their own state and hold a positive attitude.
- They are willing to take on big challenges that stretch them beyond what they currently know how to do and to ride the roller coaster of needing to continually rise to the occasion.

These entrepreneurial qualities are latent in all humans. We all have the capacity for agency and learning, for self-management, and for will. For anyone who wants to make a difference in the way businesses affect the world, this book lays out ways to make that aspiration focused and doable. Changing the game is a stretch for anyone, but this book introduces a variety of ordinary people who used their drive to make it happen. *The Responsible Entrepreneur* offers a blueprint for a new kind of business leadership.

The Responsible Entrepreneur Master Plan

In what follows, you will encounter three distinct windows into the what and how of becoming a responsible entrepreneur:

1. First, I distinguish among four different domains within which you can pursue change. These domains are organized hierarchically into four levels, each of which requires a higher level of commitment and capability than the previous one.
2. Connected to these four domains are four roles that responsible entrepreneurs can play. They are drawn from anthropological research into Native American cultures, and because they have turned out to be universal in human experience, they are described as archetypes.
3. Finally, the stories themselves introduce real business leaders whose lives and experience suggest guiding patterns from which you can invent your own playbook. They are intended to inspire and give companionship along the road.

In Part One, I introduce the archetypes and show how they support the resilience, agility, and leadership needed to accomplish significant change. Then, in Part Two, I introduce four iconic entrepreneurs, each of whom has strongly exhibited the characteristics of one of the archetypes: Steve Jobs, cofounder of Apple, adopted the Warrior; Richard Branson, founder of Virgin Companies, has worked from the Clown; Oprah Winfrey, founder of HARPO Productions, has pursued the role of Hunter; and Larry Page, cofounder of Google, Inc., has carried out the work of Headman. I discuss how each of these leaders discovered and grew into their role, becoming increasingly effective at it over time. Acknowledging their imperfections, I also explore the shadow expression of the archetype in their lives, which they must learn to reconcile in order to succeed.

Part Three unpacks the dynamic structure of each archetype—how it works and why. To illustrate, I've included the stories of ten entrepreneurs, ordinary people who have produced extraordinary results through their clarity, intention, and dedicated effort. Part Four then talks about how to put it all together, advancing on a path as a responsible entrepreneur.

Each of the entrepreneurs I worked with or interviewed for this book has publicly declared an intention to help change the world. Their efforts, as they would be the first to tell you, are works in progress, but they have also achieved significant results. Between what could and should be, and what is currently possible, lies a space of potentiality into which the responsible entrepreneur continually seeks to stretch and grow.

Business Is a Preeminent Instrument for Global Change

Occasionally entrepreneurs come along who are willing to set their sights on using business as a means to change the world. This enables them to alter the material foundation of our economy, one of the most highly leveraged places from which change arises. One of my aims at this time in my life is to encourage a tidal wave of responsible entrepreneurs, so that this way of doing business becomes the norm, not the exception.

"But," I am often asked, "isn't improving social or environmental conditions the role of philanthropy?" I believe that, as important as philanthropy is, it has been extended and pushed into arenas that are not appropriate to it. This is the direct result of the failure of businesses to take responsibility for the effects of their actions, assuming that others will address any issues created by their thoughtless practices. This is just one more version of outsourcing.

Responsible entrepreneurs see themselves as actors in systems much larger than their immediate businesses and environments. In other words, they view business itself as an instrument for change. All entrepreneurs bring something to the party, but responsible entrepreneurs pursue change on a grand scale; they are interested in more than just their own businesses or communities. They seek the bold, sweeping moves that can benefit nations, ecosystems, and the planet as a whole.

Because of this, responsible entrepreneurs can have a profound effect if they can create the right platform. This requires that they have successful businesses, which provide them with a reliable stream of resources and the credibility that comes from managing large challenges. In addition, they must recognize that innovation can serve the double purpose of securing the success of a business while simultaneously transforming the world.

A Blueprint for Responsible Entrepreneurs to Change the World

This book is filled with stories about extraordinary people who demonstrate that it *is* possible to change the game for the better. They started out like any of us. They each faced personal obstacles and setbacks, just as you and I must. But they were willing to grow themselves, and that created the people I celebrate in these pages.

I offer this book in the spirit of inspiration as much as instruction. I want it to show how business could and should play a leading role in fostering the social and ecological change that will lead to a healthier and more prosperous future for all. More important, I want it to describe the means by which any entrepreneur can aspire to and pursue this higher order of work. It is my sincere desire to engage entrepreneurs everywhere in becoming *responsible*.

Part One

Changing the World Requires Game-Changing Roles

Entrepreneurship is built into us as humans. We are wired to assume personal agency and to affect our world. Again and again in my work with businesses I have watched people come to life when they saw ways to apply their creativity to making things work. These were ordinary people who would never have thought of themselves as entrepreneurs, but all of them had entrepreneurial characteristics. Entrepreneurialism isn't for a rare few who are born to it. It is a fire waiting to be lit in all of us.

Once you have the motivation to become an entrepreneur, the challenge is to discover the method. It won't be found in online news items with titles like "The Top Five Things Successful Entrepreneurs Do Every Day!" You don't become Steve Jobs by making a to-do list.

For entrepreneurs who want to change the world (or, in Steve Jobs's words, "put a dent in the universe"), this first section lays out the basis for constructing your own roadmap. It proposes the following as levers for change:

Domains of Leverage—industries, social systems, cultural paradigms, and governance infrastructure
A System of Archetypes—for transformational leadership
Roles to Take On—how entrepreneurs bring these archetypes into the domains they choose to influence

Listen to interviews of Responsible Entrepreneurs who are *changing the world:* www.ResponsibleTrep.com/bookbonus.

1

Modern Archetypes Are Altering the Future

There is no passion to be found playing small—in settling for a life that is less than the one you are capable of living.
—NELSON MANDELA

To play the game well is one thing. To play it with style and creativity is even better. But changing the game itself is a different level of play entirely, a level that you must be willing to master if you are to advance your path as a responsible entrepreneur. Entrepreneurship frequently requires courage. This is especially true for responsible entrepreneurs, who are willing to put themselves and their resources on the line to improve the world in a significant way.

Jeffrey Hollander, the founder of Seventh Generation, was fired from his own company after almost twenty-five years at the helm. The transition required him to do some serious soul searching. He realized that, in the interest of creating better ways of doing business, he had been refusing to play the game by the old rules. But his actions, as principled and innovative as they had been, hadn't really affected how others were playing the game. With this realization, he came to understand that he needed to become a game changer.

Many entrepreneurs who set out to apply their energies to making a difference find themselves sucked into a vortex of rules that were defined by others. They can't completely escape. That's when they discover that if you want to operate from a place of creative freedom, you have to take on defining the game itself, changing the rules for everyone.

Four Domains for Changing the Game

Responsible entrepreneurs tend to focus their game-changing aspirations in one of four distinct domains:

1. *Industries*, where the work is to disrupt and replace automatic patterns with ones that are more life affirming.
2. *Social systems*, where the work is to move upstream to the causes of social problems and address them at their source.
3. *Cultural paradigms*, where the work is to make the belief systems that unconsciously govern human experience more holistic and embracing.
4. *Foundational agreements*, where the work is to renew and vitalize the deeper intention behind the governing documents, such as a corporate charter or the U.S. Constitution, that explicitly lay out the social contract by which a community or nation defines itself.

Four Timeless Leadership Archetypes Evident Everywhere Today

These four domains correspond very closely to a hierarchy of archetypal leadership roles that have been observed again and again in traditional cultures around the world. Although hidden from the awareness of most modern business people, these roles have continued to manifest themselves in modified form right up to the present day. Anthropologists and native peoples name them Warrior, Clown, Hunter, and Headman. These archetypes have long provided a structured and powerful way to evoke the leadership most needed by traditional (and modern!) communities at any given time.

1. The Warrior protects the values of a community, constantly calling people to remember what gives their lives meaning. In the world of business, this work takes place within the domain of industry.
2. The Clown pokes fun at collective self-centeredness and unconsciousness, opening space for humility and heartfelt appreciation of others. The Clown is therefore naturally called to work within the domain of social systems.
3. The Hunter perpetuates life by strengthening the mutual exchange between the tribe and the natural world. In the modern world, the Hunter's domain is cultural paradigms.
4. The Headman (or Headwoman in increasingly many cases) awakens individuals to their potential and inspires them to work with others in order to contribute to something larger than themselves. The domain of the Headman is the reorientation of people to the deeper meaning of their foundational agreements.

The four archetypes are all necessary to the healthy functioning of society, and taken together they form a whole system. If any one of them is missing, society becomes vulnerable. If the Warrior impulse is missing, conformity drives behaviors and commoditization drives economies— the opposite of the pursuit of singularity and meaning. Warriors pursue the integrity and creativity that enable a society to orient to what could be rather than settling for what already is.

If the Clown is missing, inequity and inequality become more severe. No one pays attention to the disproportionate impacts of social choices on the poor or dispossessed. No one champions the mutual bonds of obligation that maintain the integrity of the social fabric. Clowns illuminate and transform the causes of class war.

If the Hunter is missing, cultural cohesion breaks down. People identify as members of one interest group or another and lobby for their part of the pie. They lose the ability to see what the whole needs in order to maintain its integrity. Conflicting paradigms do battle over how the whole should work, as each interest group claims to speak for it and attempts to dominate it. A Hunter perspective grasps and addresses the fragmentation that underlies culture wars.

If the Headman impulse is missing, society and self-governance can't evolve. A Headman or Headwoman recognizes entropy when it sets in and intervenes to catalyze its opposite. Rather than managing symptoms, he or she works to reinspirit the community.

In traditional societies it was understood that individuals would take up one or another of these roles as needed by the tribe. Some people might have had natural gifts that predisposed them to one archetype or another, but all were expected to help fight the battles, gather the food, and sit in council to determine the direction of the community. A tribal member might naturally have moved through the different roles at different points in his or her life as a reflection of inner growth and maturity.

An Archetype Is a Mantle You Consciously Take Up

It may be helpful to note that I use the word "archetype" slightly differently from how it is customarily applied in modern psychology. For me, an archetype is a *paradigmatic pattern* that offers people a way to access something in themselves—something universal or beyond their habitual way of working and thinking. Thought of in this way, an archetype is something that one can aspire to live up to and that offers a cohesive set of beliefs about how things should or could be.

Archetypes can function as active agents in your psyche and in your interactions with the world. They can raise aspiration and encourage striving, offering a way to move beyond your existing self-image. They engender opportunities for learning, discovery, and personal growth. Perhaps most important, they enable new and unexpected ways to make a contribution.

When people point to Gandhi, Mandela, or Buddha as role models, they mean that these are exemplars of life lived according to a set of higher principles. They exhibit the exceptional realization of human potential. They are, in other words, people who have striven to live through an archetype as they engaged the world.

In order to advance and evolve, societies need members who are willing to extend themselves beyond existing norms and patterns of behavior. Individuals who take on an archetypal role provide critically important leadership that enables societies to remain vibrant, healthy, and dynamic. Often it is in periods of crisis and disruption that the need for this kind of leadership becomes most apparent. However, the choice to step into such a role is always available to people of good conscience. One eloquent example is the story of how the tribal peoples of Botswana preserved their independence from European incursions at the end of the nineteenth century and birthed a new African nation.

Archetypal Leadership and the Birth of a Nation

The modern nation of Botswana came into being as a protectorate of Britain in 1885, in order to defend its territory against the commercial and political opportunism of Cecil Rhodes and his competitors among Boer mining companies. At that time, three main tribes inhabited the region, which lies north and east of the countries now known as South Africa and Zimbabwe. A state of low-grade warfare between tribal people and European commercial interests had been decimating communities throughout southern Africa for decades, and these three tribes were beginning to experience incursions into their own territory. They could see the likely future they were facing.

One of the tribal chiefs, Khama III, was a gifted Headman. He initiated an alliance with the other two chieftains, Bathoen (a natural Hunter) and Sebele (a Clown), in order to create a shared strategy for defense. It quickly became clear that, even working together, they did not have the strength to fend off the invaders. What they were missing was a Warrior—a critical dimension if they were to maintain their independence—and they decided to invite the British government to take on this leadership and become their fourth partner.

They traveled to London to petition the queen to make Botswana a protectorate. As part of this negotiation, they secured the right to govern themselves as an independent authority while providing Britain with a railroad easement and a bulwark against the growing hegemony of Rhodes in the region. Because they were seeking a leadership partnership, Khama III had the foresight to insist on a joint council that would ensure full transparency and mutual influence—a key contributor to the long-term success of his strategy.

Each of the three tribal chiefs had a history that fueled his commitment to concerns beyond himself. This would become instrumental in the development of his unique character and his contribution to the creation of powerful founding institutions for the new nation.

In the role of Headman, as the first elected president of the new protectorate, Khama III sought to grow the governing institutions that would lead to a society free from the corrosive influence of racism. As a young man he had been sent to pursue his legal education at Oxford, but had been denied admission because of his race. While in England, he had fallen in love with a woman connected to his circle of friends. When they applied to be married as a mixed-race couple, a firestorm of controversy had erupted, not only among white English society but also among the members of his tribe. Although they eventually married, the prejudice in Botswana was so strong that Khama III had been forced to leave his wife behind when he returned home.

Thus when it came time to establish the new government of Botswana, the deep personal impact of these experiences caused Khama III to pursue the vision of a society blind to race. He designed political systems based on full democratic participation of individuals, regardless of race, heritage, entitlement, or sex.

Bathoen, the second tribal leader, focused on creating a post-tribal culture. His father, a tribal king, had died when he was a young boy. The leadership vacuum created by Bathoen's inability to step into his hereditary role had given him firsthand experience of the dynamics that create war. Everywhere he looked he saw people doing battle over fundamental resources. When he finally was installed as king, it was with a strongly held conviction that he needed to shift the traditions that generate perpetual conflict. He had immediately set out to establish common ownership of the land base, so that the tribe as a whole would benefit whenever value was generated from it.

As one of the founders of Botswana, Bathoen enshrined common ownership of the land within the constitution. When diamond deposits were discovered a year later, their ownership was secured in the name of the people. Rather than becoming the cause of tribal warfare, this shared mineral wealth fueled the rapid development of the country into a stable and prosperous democracy. Characteristically, Bathoen sought to have people identify as members of a nation rather than of a tribe. In one instance, he designed the nation's first census without a box for declaring tribal or racial ancestry—a tradition that has been preserved up to the present day.

Sebele, a Clown, wanted to create social systems that enabled full participation for everyone. This led him to establish free, universal education for Botswana. As a child, he had survived a brutal massacre by white South Africans attempting to expand their hegemony north into his tribe's territory. This had caused Sebele, a deeply religious man, to pursue a lifelong quest to understand the causes of war and to discover the means to end it. He had come to the realization that the single greatest antidote to violence was education, and with the help of missionary organizations he had begun to set up a system of schools for his tribe. His success in this effort brought him to the attention of the other founders of Botswana, who invited him to join their historic mission to London. Although Sebele died within a few years of the establishment of the protectorate, in that time he was able to create the infrastructure to extend education to all people, including girls, which provided the basis for a profoundly egalitarian society.

The integration of these four leadership styles or approaches launched a process of successful nation building that may be unique in the history of colonialism. With the threat of British military power to help secure the new nation's borders, the founders set to work embedding the values that would enable Botswana to avoid the history of instability, despotism, tribal conflict, and racism that poisoned neighboring Southern Africa for generations. Over time, this enabled Botswana to become the oldest and most stable democracy on the continent, with one of its strongest economies.

Accessing an Archetype Gives You More Choices and Power

Great power can be derived from working with living archetypes—power that can be beneficial or destructive. The destructive side of an archetype is far more likely to manifest when it is operating unconsciously. Making archetypes explicit enables leaders to develop ways of working that are consonant with an archetypal role, while avoiding its characteristic pitfalls. In the chapters that follow, I will offer a framework to help you to become less habitual and automatic about the influence of these archetypes. By understanding the core motivations and methods of each, you can exercise greater choice about how to access archetypal energies in order to drive changes in the world that express your own character and destiny.

In other words, how you use these archetypes depends on a large number of variables, about which you can exercise a great deal of conscious choice. Although most of us have a natural tendency toward or preference for one or another of these archetypes, all of us have the potential to engage with each of them as needed. First of all, the domain within which you choose to change the game is a good indicator of the archetypal energy that will be required. If the game is large enough, you may find that you will have to draw on all of the archetypes. The good news is that this doesn't have to be something you do alone. Just as the founders of Botswana understood that they needed each other to take on their great task, you too can ask for support from colleagues or peers— either to help you live up to the demands placed on you by a specific archetype or to partner with you to invoke the layered, multifaceted perspective that becomes possible when all four are present.

2

Four Game-Changing Entrepreneurial Roles

If you wish to make an apple pie from scratch, you must first invent the universe.
—CARL SAGAN

In my experience working with entrepreneurs, each of the four domains within which responsible entrepreneurs operate requires one of the four archetypes of leadership, which translate into four unique entrepreneurial roles (see Figure 2.1). The archetype required to change . . .

. . . an industry is the Warrior, and I call the corresponding entrepreneur a *realization entrepreneur*.

. . . social systems is the Clown, which in the entrepreneurial world I call a *reconnection entrepreneur*.

. . . cultural paradigms is the Hunter or *reciprocity entrepreneur*.

. . . connection to foundational agreements is the Headman or *regenerative entrepreneur*.

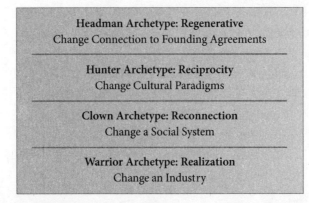

Figure 2.1   Hierarchy of Entrepreneurial Roles

The Four Entrepreneurial Roles Do Different Work

The *realization entrepreneur* is driven by the vision of an improved reality, which sources her creativity in pursuit of a better world. As a Warrior, the realization entrepreneur feels called to live up to and promote a higher, sacred intention or aspiration.

The *reconnection entrepreneur* reveals the gaps in our cognition regarding the impacts of existing social systems (such as the inequitable distribution of opportunity). As a Clown, the reconnection entrepreneur calls attention to that which is failing to flourish—in children and families, in communities, or in ecosystems—and helps people become self-conscious enough to make the situation right.

A *reciprocity entrepreneur* is concerned with the effects of business on all of the players in a system and is driven to ensure balance between what is taken and what is given. The reciprocity entrepreneur is oriented toward wholeness and instinctively pursues the kind of reciprocally beneficial stakeholder relationships that I described in my previous book, *The Responsible Business*. As a Hunter, the reciprocity entrepreneur is particularly good at helping point out interdependencies and dynamic effects: among people, between people and nature, and among behaviors and beliefs.

Finally, the *regenerative entrepreneur* seeks to reveal and evolve the inherent potential of the founding agreements that create the accepted structures within which society operates. The regenerative entrepreneur goes back to the foundational agreements that give birth to a society or an organization, bringing new life and understanding to what those agreements mean and how they could become more deeply manifest. As a form of Headman, the regenerative entrepreneur disrupts, upgrades, reimagines, and evolves institutions and institutionalized agreements, which makes it possible for people to come together and work in more powerful ways toward more inspiring ends.

In addition to goods and services, each of the four entrepreneurial roles also brings unique inspirational value to the world:

- The realization entrepreneur is a reminder of the importance of personal agency, of dreams, and of getting to the essence of things.
- The reconnection entrepreneur is a reminder of the generosity of the human spirit, the importance of caring about more than oneself, and the fact that good businesses can operate from conscience.
- Reciprocity entrepreneurs provide a window into the complex and living interrelatedness of the world and the inseparability of business actions from their effects on wholeness.
- Regenerative entrepreneurs demonstrate that humans can beneficially disrupt and evolve their social and ecological systems to be more deeply supportive of life itself.

Responsible Entrepreneurs Take on American Society and Social Equity

One way to help clarify the distinctions among these archetypes is to see how each would bring a different approach to a particular topic; for example, challenges and opportunities arising from the current pattern of income distribution.

If a realization entrepreneur wanted to address inequities in peoples' ability to earn, she might go to work to transform the standards for income distribution within her company as a way to build a platform for transforming her industry. For example, she might introduce profit sharing as a means to improve opportunity for all members of her company by enabling them to benefit directly from the improvement of the business's products and services. She would then clearly articulate the principles that everyone in the company would live up to and promote those principles actively within the industry at large.

A reconnection entrepreneur tends to look beyond his industry when addressing questions of income distribution and to identify the source of the problem within a system that needs to be evolved. For example, a reconnection entrepreneur might see that education is core to shifting inequitable patterns of income distribution. He could set out to establish linkages between business and educational systems (for example, through internships or tuition and job guarantees) in order to enable everyone in society to participate successfully in the economy. He might determine that the system itself promotes inequity and thus work on the redesign of education. Alternatively, he might work on building entrepreneurial capacity among disadvantaged communities so that they could successfully use his products in their own small businesses.

A reciprocity entrepreneur exposes and confronts beliefs that cause some people or groups to be seen as inferior and therefore unworthy of full participation in income-producing roles. She would work to shift income distribution by directly engaging people who are disadvantaged in realizing their own inherent potential, thus challenging or disproving beliefs about their inherent inferiority. She might build capability among women or people of color or disabled people and then promote individuals from these groups into leadership roles as a means to improve the company's performance. She might redesign products and services to provide the kind of access to the instruments of society (such as food choices, health care, transportation, communications, banking, land tenure, and tools) that enable disadvantaged communities to improve their lives. She might foster the development of minority-owned businesses among her suppliers and her distributors. And she would proudly promote this work (and differentiate her business) as an example of what a truly equitable society should look like.

A regenerative entrepreneur works on the structures and institutions that dictate what is possible. From his perspective, income inequality is shaped and fostered by the legal codes and institutional practices that limit who can participate and how, thereby favoring the few who can master the complexities involved and excluding everyone else. He would therefore go to work on closing the gap between what the core purpose and possibility of an economic system really is and how its potential is currently limited by the way we choose to govern it. He would look at the institutions that he has to interface with as a successful businessperson and ask why they were established and how they would need to work if they were reconceived as being for the good of all. He would ask where he could take advantage of the way these institutions are structured in order to move them toward a more ideal way of pursuing their objectives. Instead of taking advantage of his knowledge for his own gain, he would ask how to take advantage of that knowledge in order to benefit everyone—finding loopholes that could be used for a greater social purpose. He might seek to open up the investment process to allow anyone to participate in the possibility of ownership. He might seek to increase the transparency required by regulatory agencies by holding his suppliers to a higher degree of transparency with regard to the social or environmental impacts of their decisions. He might invent new structures (such as new forms of governance for corporations) that provide an alternate path for the future evolution of broader social institutions.

Four Big Promises

Essentially, a responsible entrepreneur is prepared to make a big promise: to change the game by changing the way his business plays it. Let's look at how this promise plays out in each of the four domains.

A Realization Entrepreneur Promises to Transform Industries

An industry can be defined and understood in terms of shared stakeholders and value-adding processes. For example, all of the companies in a given industry will draw on the same populations of suppliers, resources, technologies, and customers or consumers. These are shared dynamics for everyone in each particular industry. A realization entrepreneur influences an industry by profoundly changing one or more of these core dynamics, making the old way of conceiving the industry obsolete. An example of how this can be done is by introducing a dimension that previously had not been seen as fundamental to the industry.

Steve Jobs, cofounder of Apple, had a core insight that user-friendliness depended on a combination of aesthetics and integrated utility. This allowed Apple to create a series of elegant offerings whose simplicity and accessibility enabled them to displace a whole range of other products. For example, after the iPhone was introduced, within less than a year it had changed the way people all over the world communicated. This not only forced the cell phone industry to turn on a dime in order to compete but also impacted a host of other industries. By introducing a phone that was capable of running apps, Apple made other products and technologies—from cameras and portable music devices to landlines and maps—either redundant or obsolete.

For a realization entrepreneur, influence comes from making people's lives better. A realization entrepreneur recognizes that an industry has the responsibility to ensure that people can make choices and pursue aspirations without having to face compromises imposed on them by the industry's lack of imagination. Steve Jobs didn't think of the people he was serving as consumers; he thought of them as human beings. This enabled Apple to understand that people weren't buying products so much as they were buying access to a new kind of freedom and power in interactions with their worlds.

Core to changing an industry—the door through which a realization entrepreneur must enter—is the imperative to wake it up to the next level of potential that it could be delivering to its customers. This is fundamental to business responsibility, and it provides the platform and credibility from which other kinds of responsibility can emerge.

A Reconnection Entrepreneur Promises to Transform Social Systems That Define Behaviors

Social systems limit the expression of individuals, institutions, and society as a whole by defining what behaviors are or aren't acceptable. Some examples include the education system, which determines what kinds of knowledge are important and therefore who has access to opportunity; the welfare system, which decides who qualifies for help and how it is paid for; and transit systems, which dictate how hard or easy it is (especially for disadvantaged people) to move around and lead a functional life.

. Systems and the procedures that flow from them are what define, bound, and maintain a society. They point to and enforce what are considered appropriate patterns of behavior. Because they are ubiquitous, they define social norms that come to be perceived as truth. A society draws on shared language, etiquette, and other signifiers to enable shared understanding. This facilitates the smooth operation of social interaction. The problem is that these same signifiers also proscribe what is possible for people to pursue on a daily basis, shutting down the possibilities for both innovation and exchange. Without these possibilities humans cannot thrive.

A reconnection entrepreneur influences society by overtly and creatively challenging flawed social systems, exposing their institutionalized behavioral norms and unfair outcomes. He builds a bridge to a new pattern by taking into account all that is missing from the current system and then demonstrating a beneficial alternative. This is an important aspect of the character of a reconnection entrepreneur: he wants people to believe in the alternative because they have been able to see it, experience it, and recognize its inherent value. To be successful at this, he must show how the new way of doing things improves opportunities for reciprocal exchange for all members of the system.

Elon Musk, the libertarian founder of PayPal, SpaceX, and Tesla Motors, believed that the capitalist system was working exactly as it was supposed to when, in the early 1990s, Toyota and General Motors formed a joint venture to develop an electric car designed to address California's highly restrictive pollution standards. Brought out in 1996, the EV-1 car sold rapidly, demonstrating that the market could determine what was really needed. But only two years later, a new governor succeeded in rolling back carbon emission standards, and General Motors begin to recall and crush all of the new cars. Musk reported later that it felt like his own dreams were being crushed. There was a great market, a working technology, but GM stopped the electric car in its tracks. Within a week, Musk decided to build his own electric car.

At the age of thirteen, Musk had a revelatory vision of three technological advances that would help humans create a healthier world. The first was the Internet, which would level the playing field for innovation. The second was sustainable energy, which would eliminate the need to despoil the planet. The third was space exploration, which would open new opportunities for life on other planets. As a youthful idealist, he believed these breakthroughs were imminent and would be achieved within five years. As an adult, his understanding has deepened, and he has placed his attention on shifting the social systems that keep destructive or limiting patterns in place. Even so, it is still possible to see his early vision playing out in his wide-ranging businesses and investments.

The Tesla Motors car is intended to work on energy sustainability by leveraging the transportation industry, thereby reflecting back to us a new image of who we could be as a society. Musk's strategy seeks to improve the safety of transportation, its impact on the planet, and the limitations it places on people's life choices. He has subverted car safety standards by outperforming them. In one instance, his car body proved so strong that it broke the machinery designed to test its resistance to being crushed. He has also innovated with regard to how people buy cars. For example, he circumvented Texas laws instituted to favor car dealers by setting up auto showrooms designed as galleries, where people could visit and experience the cars without buying them and then order them online from another state. (This is such a characteristic reconnection entrepreneur move, beautifully demonstrating the Clown or Trickster archetype at work!)

With regard to energy, Musk has radically upgraded the performance of electric cars by improving their mileage, range, and maneuverability, while setting the stage for them to be entirely powered from renewable sources.

Although over time these innovations will undoubtedly have a powerful impact on the automobile industry, Musk is not driven by this aim. When he started Tesla he knew nothing about designing cars. He pursued it because he saw that it would be an effective way to work on a greater social evolution. As a reconnection entrepreneur, he wanted to show how it is possible to intentionally and beneficially evolve social systems, rather than only argue about how the car industry should change.

A Reciprocity Entrepreneur Promises to Transform Culture

Cultures include collective beliefs and assumptions. Tribes and nations are held together by cosmologies—that is, their implicit and explicit beliefs about how the world works. Cosmologies lend themselves to becoming dogmas, becoming the "one and only way" to interpret what is right and good. They define inclusion and exclusion, success and punishment. They very easily become invisible and unconscious when we become certain that "that's just how the world is." Reciprocity entrepreneurs seek to open up and evolve these sets of beliefs.

In practice, the reciprocity entrepreneur seeks to avoid conversations about right and wrong, true and false. Instead, she evokes reflection on the effect and impact of cultural beliefs and assumptions. She goes right out to the edge of current boundaries and asks what is beyond them. Before she comes to her own conclusions, she invites other people to join her and look at the implications. Once there is a vision in place, she helps make it real and understandable and in so doing extends and evolves the cultural cosmology.

A reciprocity entrepreneur is driven to look at where the blockages are in society and to ask how cultural beliefs and boundaries contribute to creating and continuing the disorder. She also looks at thwarted aspirations, the situations in which individuals and communities continue against all odds to pursue something different. Her work is to serve as an instrument for making the negative consequences of cultural assumptions apparent to everyone. It is the nature of this archetype to open people up, making them more conscious of the places where culturally determined beliefs cause pain and blockage in their own lives. This sets the stage for a larger questioning of cultural assumptions.

The opportunity to transform cultural paradigms sometimes manifests through an inspiring story about those who have succeeded in removing barriers and extending boundaries. Storytelling can become an instrument for evolving cultural agreements. When Oprah Winfrey began her evolution as a reciprocity entrepreneur, she made this shift from stories that revealed the underlying cultural dynamics in the struggles experienced by her guests to a narrative about who we can all become. Her new message was, "We need you for who you are. You matter with regard to what we need to change."

A Regenerative Entrepreneur Promises to Transform Our Understanding of the Foundational Agreements by Which We Govern Ourselves

Foundational agreements tend to structure our decisions and actions and our ability to realize the inherent potential in any organized entity (including societies, businesses, and families). These agreements are the hardest domain to influence because they are so instrumental in bringing our institutions into existence. They become almost invisible to us as they take on an aura of eternal necessity.

This domain can be evolved only through overt and disruptive intervention. The right intervention at the right moment can suddenly cause everyone to question the validity of a particular structure or the way it is being administered. Such an intervention creates a new precedent, which shifts what everyone can see is possible. The U.S. federal court system, which operates both within and upon precedent, is an example of how the systemic transformation of founding agreements can be created.

Interventions at this level tend to offer simultaneously the vision and lived experience of a different future. Pulling this off requires power and cleverness, and without the right level of authority and credibility, a regenerative entrepreneur won't be able to persuade people even to attempt this level of restructuring. He must have secured for himself the legitimacy that would allow him to introduce these disruptions, and he must be prepared to move from one governance stream to another (for example, from policymakers or administrators to the courts, or vice versa) to make his point or advance his game-changing strategy.

Accessing the full power of this archetype takes a lifetime of practice (although it can be approached by anyone on a more limited scale). Regenerative leadership is a calling that tends to show early in a person's life, usually in response to systems and processes that seem to be directly destructive to the future potential of a nation or community. It demands the will to examine oneself personally and to be utterly transparent, to make one's intentions evident and trustworthy. The regenerative entrepreneur does not engage in power plays. His work has to do with increasing the field of opportunity for everyone.

J. I. Rodale, visionary founder and so-called "mad prophet" of the organic food movement, set out to transform the way human beings interacted with the most fundamental infrastructure of all: the soil, water, and microbial life that allow us to derive sustenance from Earth. In 1930, through his family-owned business, Rodale Press, he began to create a publishing empire that advocated for a completely new and holistic vision of what it means to sustain health—for people and for our planet Earth.

In the beginning, his vision expressed itself as a backyard gardening, do-it-yourself phenomenon. Later it was picked up and extended by his son, Robert, who helped mainstream the ideas and practices of organic farming, gardening, and holistic personal health, and pioneered a body of thought and writing on the topic of regeneration. Under his stewardship, Rodale Press became one of the most successful publishers in the world.

Rodale's work not only set out to transform the industries of agriculture, food, and health (a process that is still under way) but also explicitly sought to transform the systems, culture, and governing infrastructure for how we grow and handle our food, and Rodale Press gave him a very powerful platform from which to do so. The power of organic certification, which has helped drive a global movement toward organic farming methods, is probably its most evident effect, as shown by the resistance it created among large industrial agriculture companies when it was put in place by the USDA.

Part of the appeal of the Rodale story is how a small, quirky family succeeded in changing the world, and how their pervasive influence continues to unfold even as the name is no longer a household word.

They have sourced a profound change in thinking, which continues to grow around the world.

Taking on a Game-Changing Role Matters

There are long-standing arguments in academic literature about whether business people should be managers or leaders. Some authors advocate abandoning the managing role altogether. Others claim that the key to leadership is management. The emerging consensus is that, depending on circumstances, both roles are necessary (along with additional roles, such as that of planner). To have a full and effective life, you need the agility and skill to move easily among multiple roles. In the same way, to be effective as a game changer, you must be able to choose and play the role that is appropriate to the situation.

The roles I have described here are powerful because they are derived from an archetypal source. By asking ourselves, "What would Buddha do? Or Martin Luther King?" we are seeking a source of energy that can uplift, instruct, and inform us about our options. Putting ourselves in the shoes of these exemplars provides us with perspective and inspiration, and challenges us to become more skilled at the methods they used. Archetypal roles provide a roadmap for taking on bigger challenges, making bigger promises, and focusing the energy and resources needed to get bigger results.

Part Two
The Secret Structure Behind the Approach of Four Iconic Entrepreneurs

Up to this point, the domains, archetypes, and roles that I've introduced have for the most part remained general and abstract. By contrast, this section is devoted to stories of real people. I want to show how the idea of an archetype or an entrepreneurial role comes alive when it takes on flesh and blood.

For these stories, I've chosen four iconic entrepreneurs—business leaders who are loved by some, loathed by others. I've chosen them because their stories, while generally well known, have never been examined in terms of the archetypal patterns they reveal. How do icons become iconic? Is it because they represent something exemplary to us, something archetypal, much as religious icons are intended to represent some aspect of the sacred? What motivates them? What gives them their drive?

For all the power of the idea of archetype, it's important to remember that we are not archetypes; we're human beings. In the stories that follow, I invite you to investigate whether it is possible to see these archetypal energies at work in my chosen exemplars and then, maybe, in yourself. Remember that each of my entrepreneurial icons is a human being with a strong personality and publicly visible feet of clay. My point is not that they or their companies are perfect, but that they have been profoundly influential through their embodiment of an archetypal pattern of thinking and working that is greater than their personalities. Because of this, they have been pioneers in the field of responsible entrepreneurship, and their examples are instructive for anyone who chooses to use business as an instrument for creating a better world.

Listen to interviews of Responsible Entrepreneurs who are *changing the world:* www.ResponsibleTrep.com/bookbonus.

3

Steve Jobs and the Role of the Realization Entrepreneur

So let's not use a stylus. We're going to use the best pointing device in the world. We're going to use a pointing device that we're all born with—born with ten of them. It works like magic.
—STEVE JOBS

Realization entrepreneurs understand that when we go on autopilot, we lose connection to reality and to life because we are not present to what is unfolding right in front of us. As a manifestation of the Warrior archetype, the realization entrepreneur strives to bring out the best in people, in things, and in business itself, in order to make us more honorable, more loyal, more conscientious, and more true to our nature.

In this context, realization has a dual meaning. First, it means coming to understand something new, yet inherently true, about a subject. The second, related meaning has to do with revealing what is real about something, what is unique and singular about it and therefore connected to its essence. This revelation can open the door to discovering entirely new possibilities for what could be brought into existence. A realization entrepreneur acts to express that new understanding through her products or services. This impulse manifests itself as a drive toward perfection, and as higher orders of perfection show up in her offerings, they tend to transform how an entire industry thinks about itself and its offerings.

Realization entrepreneurs are motivated to:

- *Get to the essence of things, because that's where reality lies.* The Warrior archetype is associated with honor and integrity, but within these qualities is a drive to stay connected to a deep and accurate understanding of reality. A Warrior, to play her role, has to understand the situation in front of her, right now, in the present moment.

- *Activate the creativity that is possible when people become self-managing.* Warriors, for better or for worse, expect everyone to share their commitment to integrity and responsibility, in part because they know that when truly self-accountable people come together, they are able to push each other to extraordinary levels of creative breakthrough.

- *Invent products and services that make life work better.* Contribution and service is at the core of the Warrior archetype. In the life of a realization entrepreneur, this manifests as an unrelenting commitment to helping customers pursue their aspirations more successfully.

Build a Platform to Make a Difference

Steve Jobs said that there were three points in his life that formed who he became. The first was learning that he had been adopted. The second was being fired from Apple, the company he coconceived and built. The third was being diagnosed with cancer. It was in being fired by Apple that Jobs discovered the motivation to make a comeback and the means by which to change the world.

Soon after leaving Apple, Jobs founded NeXT, where he demonstrated a coalescence of the art and science of computer design that could be directly experienced by the user. He considered this to be of particular importance to education because of the power of visual communication to enable user participation (a classic example of striving to serve the aspirations of users). During this period he also acquired the computer graphics division of Lucasfilm, which he developed into Pixar. Pixar's innovations represented a breakthrough in the digital generation of moving images and immediately changed the movie industry.

When Jobs returned to Apple eleven years later, he drew from these two entrepreneurial endeavors to create a platform for changing the computer industry. Soon designers, engineers, or artists could use Apple products to make their ideas vivid and technically easy to produce, and Apple entered a fertile period of innovation and growth.

Essence of the iPad: One Hand Scoopability

Jobs was a notorious perfectionist. Or at least that is how he was perceived. But viewed from the perspective of a Warrior archetype, he was actually focused on essence, not perfection. Essence was the guide to his perspective, and his gift for discerning essence allowed him to see possibilities that no one else could.

Jobs revered simplicity, a value he learned as a young man from his studies with a Zen teacher. But he pursued simplicity through essentializing rather than simplifying. Simplifying means removing whatever a thing can function without. Essentializing means starting with the heart of the thing and adding nothing that is not an aspect of that heart. For Steve Jobs, reality was found in essence, and he built everything out from his experience of essence. The image he held of the core of whatever he was working on drove his relentless perfecting of its manifestation. This same image was also the source of the famous "Jobs's reality distortion field"— where the strength of his convictions altered people's experience of reality.

Walter Isaacson, in his biography of Jobs, tells an illuminating story. Jobs and his design partner, Jonathan Ive, were working together one day when they simultaneously grasped the essence of the electronic notepad. As they reviewed several early prototypes, Jobs half unconsciously tried to pick up a device with one hand. He was instinctively seeking to scoop it up, as if it were a pad of paper. This, they realized, was the essence of the project: one-handed movement, *scoopability*. Up until that point, the engineers had been adding features and buttons that made the scoop motion hard to do. Once they understood the essence, their focus became clear.[1] Because Jobs was accustomed to looking for essence, he was able to recognize it when it presented itself.

Making Life Work Better

Jobs's adoptive father was a mechanic who loved working with his hands. One day young Steve was painting a fence with him. Years later, he reported that his father had worked with as much care on the back of the fence (which was mostly hidden by shrubbery) as the front. He addressed this simple task with an attention to detail that Jobs would later call artistic. When asked why it mattered to carefully paint something that would never be seen, his father explained that it demonstrated to you and others how dedicated you were to doing it perfectly.

This experience introduced Jobs to the multiple dimensions that could be involved in a task—an insight that would later become core to how he generated products and services designed to make life work better. He paid attention to the full experience of users, which encompassed not only function but also aesthetics and the ease with which an operation could be integrated into their lives. It's true that Jobs was engaged in a perfecting process, but it was one driven by the consumer's experience rather than his own compulsions.

Jobs sought to embed this attention to customer experience deep into the culture of Apple. At Apple University, employees used internal case studies to learn a decision-making process based on two complementary principles: first, design every product according to a rigorously developed understanding of how it will be used by customers; second, focus on a few things at a time. The idea was to encourage bold moves that would deliver key changes to make life more productive and also more exciting.

Integration and Control: Two Complementary Sides of a Contradictory Personality

As a student in the 1970s, Steve Jobs attended Reed College in Portland, Oregon, for one semester. Finding college too lifeless, he left to travel around Asia in search of spiritual insight. His seven months on the road taught him two lessons that influenced all his subsequent endeavors. From the Hindus and the Buddhists he learned that intuition must be woven into rational thought. From his Zen teachers, he learned that simplicity was the ultimate sophistication.

This outlook enabled Jobs to reconcile a host of seeming contradictions, creating a deeply integrated product line and company. For example, he insisted that imagination and engineering needed to be seamless. In his mind there was no point in having a functioning device that had no beauty, because both were important to the whole experience. Design, production, and marketing were seen as different aspects of a single activity, and Jobs's tenacity with regard to the integration of the whole of the business is often credited as the greatest source of Apple's success. Imperfections were eliminated by bringing every aspect of the process under one roof.

Many people fail to recognize the centrality and significance of this integrative quality of Jobs's character. For example, in a retrospective piece on his life, *Wired* magazine observed, "Jobs was a Buddhist, but also a tyrant." He was known for criticizing people, picking on the smallest details of their work, calling them names, and swearing at them. Some people thrived in this environment, but many withered and left. When his authorized biographer asked him why he chose to be so cruel and to risk losing talented people, his answer was, "I only want to work with people who demand perfection."

I imagine that Jobs would have responded to his detractors by saying, "It is because I'm a Buddhist that I am a tyrant." From a Zen perspective, one is not responsible for other people's reactions. When he was harsh, he assumed that the other party would take responsibility for using the interaction for personal growth. That was how he was treated by his Buddhist teachers, who confronted him sternly as a way to awaken him to the gaps in his consciousness. Just as the Buddhist teacher expected students to learn to manage their reactions as part of their work, Jobs held the same view of employees. (Whether he was skillful in his interactions is a different question.) Until one can see that the harshness and the caring were integrated, I believe one hasn't really understood Steve Jobs. He was toughest on the people he cared about and counted on—a characteristically Warrior way to be.

Jobs also had a reputation for being controlling. His need for control was driven by a belief that he was the only one who could make the mental match between the essence of a device or software and its manifestation. This was the source of his critiques: he saw essence that others could not see. The *source* of his tendency to be controlling, however, was his inability to teach others this fundamental capability. He probably never understood that essence-based thinking was a learnable capability, and this fed into his intolerance of people who weren't able to do the mental gymnastics he was good at. This was unfortunate, given how many of such people a company like Apple needs. Knowing no other way to grow them in the people around him, Jobs resorted to screaming and humiliation in the hope that it would lead (just as it had in his own Zen practice) to breakthroughs.

Jonathan Ive, Jobs's primary creative collaborator in the later years, acknowledges that being steady in the face of relentless critique was something he had to work on. He realized early in the working relationship that most people (including himself) want to be liked and have a hard time being direct when criticizing shoddy work. From his Buddhist practice, Jobs had learned to be imperturbable in the face of criticism and destabilization. He pushed for this level of equanimity in those around him so that they could drill down to find the most precise realization of a product's or service's potential. This, he believed, was what gave Apple the power to cross industries and boundaries in order to make extraordinary products.

It is interesting to note that Jobs did not humiliate people in private. For him, every meeting was a full dress parade, and every idea was inspected by the commanding officer. It was an occasion to build character, honor success, and reprimand slipshodness. Being called to account was a way to educate everyone. Being held accountable was a way to enable everyone to experience the real meaning of freedom.

As a realization entrepreneur, Jobs manifested extraordinary tenacity in his drive to perfect Apple's offerings. He wanted customers to have an experience that evoked the creativity and inspiration to express themselves more perfectly. He hated the idea of brainstorming (which engages "free" association), because it led people away from the source of real discovery, which for Jobs lay in essence. He wasn't looking for a million ideas. He wanted people to anchor themselves in a focused way to the image of something's effectiveness when being used. This was realization as concentration, the creative act of working from reality-based restraints.

4

Richard Branson and the Role of the Reconnection Entrepreneur

The responsibility for me is to invest in creating new businesses, create jobs, employ people, and to put money aside to tackle issues where we can make a difference.

—RICHARD BRANSON

Reconnection entrepreneurs seek to connect people to the meaning and the impact of their choices and actions. Put another way, they reconnect us to our consciences. This reconnection happens when we become emotionally engaged and can see that we can and must do something because we are part of the problem. As a manifestation of the Clown archetype, the reconnection entrepreneur tends to use humor, surprise, or theatricality as a way to invite us to see our own culpability. His approach isn't to accuse or to judge, but to enable us to laugh at our own blind spots.

The reconnection entrepreneur cares deeply about changing social norms, the patterns governing behavior and how people relate to one another. These norms are intended to facilitate the functioning and civility of social life, but they easily become fixed, unquestioned, and eventually unconscious. The reconnection entrepreneur works to awaken conscience, which allows us to question our underlying motives and seek a better path.

Reconnection entrepreneurs are motivated to:

- *Defy authority to create a level playing field.* An easily recognizable trait of the Clown archetype is its willingness to disrupt, to shake things up. At its best, this trait is directed to correcting power imbalances that prevent people from being able to fully participate and contribute.
- *Tease people into seeing the elephant in the room.* Clowns invite us to wake up, to see what's obvious but invisible to us. They sincerely believe that once something is brought to consciousness, a shift in behavior will naturally follow.
- *Treat the world as a neighbor.* The Clown archetype has its roots in the experience of fellowship with humanity and all living things. This evokes a profound sense of caring, for the Clown and for those moved by his comic eloquence, that extends far beyond his immediate circles of acquaintance.

At the age of twenty-three, Richard Branson was arrested and imprisoned for tax evasion. Branson, a reconnection entrepreneur, had cofounded Virgin Records a year or two earlier, while living in a London basement with a friend. His dramatic rise to become one of the world's richest and most famous entrepreneurs was still a few years in the future.

In the beginning Virgin Records was mail order only and was dependent on the British postal service for deliveries. When postal employees went on strike, Branson had less than a week to figure out how to cover salaries and expenses. Faced with the sudden collapse of his business, Branson was enticed by an illegal loophole that he couldn't resist. He had received an unexpected order from Belgium for a large number of records, enough to prevent closing his doors. So he borrowed a van and drove to the Dover ferry, where his papers were stamped confirming that the records were being exported and therefore not subject to British tax. But he discovered that he was going to have to pay tax in France, so he turned around. Then it dawned on him that he had a vanload of "exported" records that could be sold tax-free to the domestic market. Three trips like this and he could be out of debt.

Before he could take the third trip, he got a call from a friend warning him that the customs and excise people had a warrant to inspect his stock, which contained records marked with an invisible "E" for export that could be read with an ultraviolet lamp. With friends, he sorted out all of the marked records and tried to hide them in a warehouse. But the customs officials found the warehouse containing hundreds of records with the incriminating E.

Branson was arrested and taken to Dover. Sitting in his cell, it suddenly hit him that he had been stealing money from Customs. Until that moment, he had envisioned himself as a wily trickster (one of the manifestations of the Clown) eluding the snares of authority. "Only criminals get arrested," he thought to himself, and then he said out loud, "I'm guilty." Branson felt an inner door open. He vowed never again to engage in any kind of business dealings for which he would have reason to be embarrassed.

"Ever since that one night in that Dover prison, I've never been tempted to break my vow," he reported later. Because what the officials were interested in was the tax, he got out of prison by agreeing to pay £15,000 immediately and a fine of £45,000 in three installments over the next three years. This was three times the illegal profit that Virgin had made by avoiding the purchase tax. His parents had to mortgage their house to cover the initial payment. In addition to this debt, he knew that he had incurred a moral debt to his parents that would have to be repaid as well.

In time Virgin Records took off, first as a record store and then as a record label, which became known for discovering and fostering unique voices. Branson says that when he sold Virgin Records to raise the money for Virgin Airlines, he lost a part of his soul. The business had taught him so many life lessons.

Selling Your Soul for Good Outcomes

Virgin now owns over two hundred businesses, and Branson has continued to deepen his engagement with the role of reconnection entrepreneur. A story connected to Virgin's rail line is revealing in this regard. Branson was vacationing in rural Switzerland when he got a call about an accident involving a Virgin train in a remote mountainous region in northwest England. He responded immediately, knowing what the possible human toll of such an accident might be. He took the first available flight that would get him as close to the crash site as possible. This required a five-hour taxi ride to Zurich, during which he couldn't help but picture disaster. Even on flat stretches of track, a train wreck can kill hundreds and injure many more.

From the outset, Branson had set very high aspirations for Virgin Rail. He wanted to design its Pendolino trains to be unique. A strong conscience and sense of stewardship for human and natural communities (the world as neighbor) compelled him to insist that they be the safest and most environmentally friendly trains ever built. He observed that, although on the face of it trains are less polluting than airplanes, poor performance and poor ridership on English rail lines made them environmentally disastrous and actually encouraged air travel. Talk about an elephant in the room!

Branson made the deficiencies in the rail system visible by showing definitively that they didn't need to be that way. Virgin's Pendolino trains are fuel-efficient and employ a regenerative braking system (the same one used in the Toyota Prius) that generates power every time the brake is used. They also use a lightweight aircraft-type aluminum body shell. The result is 78 percent less CO_2 emissions per passenger than a flight over an equivalent distance.

Branson also insisted on the safest possible train. In his autobiography, he writes, "I wanted a train that should be able to survive an accident at full speed, regardless of cause, and the passengers should be able to walk away from it. It was a very tall order, but I didn't see why it couldn't be achieved. It was the right thing to do. Passengers are entitled to know all that can be done has been done to ensure their safety."[1]

His engineers made protection of human life their guiding principle. The linkages between the carriages, the design of the carriages themselves, the interior fittings, even the design of the windows were reconceived in terms of the contribution they could make to safety. The carriages employed monocoque construction to reduce train accidents; the engineers tried to design out every flaw that had contributed to people dying.

When Branson arrived on the crash site in northwest England, he found that it was the rails that had failed, not his train. The train had left the track airborne, then plummeted into a ravine and rolled twice. The police were astonished that it was so remarkably intact and that the level of survivorship was so high. No one died as a direct result of the accident (though one elderly woman passenger died afterward of heart failure when she visited her injured children in the hospital). Of the twenty-five injuries reported, none were life-threatening, and only eleven passengers were still in the hospital a day after the accident. The most serious injuries were sustained by the engineer, who, as the train careened downhill, refused to move back into the protection of the main body, but stayed at his station trying to maintain control.

The media insisted that the survival rate was a miracle. But from Branson's perspective it was the rational result of good design. His team planned for every eventuality and made no compromises with regard to the solutions. Doing this, Branson maintains, one can build unprecedented levels of safety (his driving aim) into any transport system. In his autobiography, he reports having to fight the government "to allow us to build our Pendolino trains to higher specifications than mandated. If you look at the health and safety regulations in Britain, the Virgin Pendolino surpasses the regulatory minimums for system safety by a factor of three."

Responsibility Starts Early and Goes on Forever

Virgin Rail had built conscience directly into the manufacturing process. Under its contract, the manufacturer got half of the money for building the train and the other half over the life of the train for safely maintaining it. This rewarded pride of workmanship and gave the manufacturer a direct stake in making choices it could stand behind. In the case of the major accident just described, only two of the almost fifty coaches were damaged enough to be taken out of service.

Branson's commitment to a life lived from a strong sense of conscience was seeded at an early age. His mother was determined that her children would be both independent and willing to be of service to their community. Shortly before Branson's twelfth birthday, she handed him a sack lunch and directed him to take his bicycle and make his way to the home of his aunt in Bournemouth, almost fifty miles distant. He was instructed to find water along the way. Setting off without directions, he had to find a route by engaging neighbors and passersby. Once in Bournemouth, he realized he didn't know his aunt's last name and had to puzzle out how to find her by asking for help from locals he didn't know.

Branson did eventually find his aunt and spent several days with her. His trip home was much simpler, and he looked forward to resting and playing when he got there. When he pedaled into the yard, his mother said, "Well done Ricky, was that fun?" Then, "Now run along to the vicar's. He's got some logs that need chopping, and I told him you'd be back any minute."

"We did this kind of work every day for our neighbors and none of it was considered charity," Branson reports. "It was all part of being in a community." When he was in his mother's orbit he was "expected to be busy, and if I tried to escape helping a neighbor by saying I had something to do, I was told I was selfish. As a result, I grew up putting other people first."

Defiance Is a Path to Conscience

In the Branson family, boys were sent to boarding school when they were twelve, on the assumption that it would build character and make men of them. School was a lonely time for Branson, who was close to his family. He turned out to be dyslexic and did poorly in class. This was a prep school, and students who did poorly were assumed to be stupid or lazy and were beaten for both. Branson had trouble reading and often had great difficulty remembering both written materials and mathematical formulas. The environment was cruel, but his parents had always told him that he had to find a way around failure. Lacking more conventional intellectual resources, he found himself using his intuition and imagination while everyone else was studying for exams. In such an environment, it was probably inevitable that Branson's Clown-like tendency to defy authority would come to fruition.

His first act of defiance was subtle. The school built leadership by encouraging students to participate in student government and to bring ideas to the attention of the headmaster. His first suggestion was to overturn the requirement that those who did not play in football matches (approximately 450 students) be required to watch them. He successfully proposed that they be chartered instead to do something useful (such as cleaning windows) rather than watching others achieve something.

Branson soon realized that there were alternatives to many of the ideas that the school held sacrosanct, and he set to work finding ways to change school rules to his benefit. With his friend Johnny Gems he launched one of his first businesses, an alternative magazine called *The Student*, which was eventually distributed in high schools and universities across England. It was filled with interviews from the uprisings of the 1960s, as well as up-and-coming musicians like John Lennon and Paul McCartney. Branson left school without completing his letters, with the idea that he could be a publisher. He was not yet seventeen when he said goodbye to his headmaster, whose parting words were, "Congratulations Branson. I predict that you will either go to prison or become a millionaire."

Branson says, "I proved him right on both counts."

As a reconnection entrepreneur, Richard Branson has demonstrated the possibility for big business to move forward a social agenda on a grand scale. In fact, he has spoken often about how business has more power than philanthropy does to bring about the deepest changes. His characteristic orientation, to address the gaps or shortfalls around him, was learned at an early age from his mother, who wanted him to be aware of his neighbors and provide them the assistance they needed. As an adult, Branson continues to be motivated by his conscience to address the underlying causes of society's ills. He sees this as the natural outcome of his business activity, and although he holds business success as a necessary threshold to enter the game, his real interest is in the change that business can engender.

5

Oprah Winfrey and the Role of the Reciprocity Entrepreneur

Doing the best at this moment puts you in the best place for the next moment.

—OPRAH WINFREY

The reciprocity entrepreneur seeks to bring about greater wholeness in individuals and cultures by exposing and transforming their belief systems. If this work is left undone, wholeness remains unattainable, because unexamined beliefs tend to split off parts of ourselves and parts of our communities. It is important to remember that these split-off parts are an illusion, a product of our perception. "Whole" and "part" are concepts through which humans seek to understand and manage their worlds. But the universe and our sensory experience of it is an immersive and seamless totality. The *wholeness* or *partness* of a thing depends on our ability to think about it separate from that seamless totality.

In this context, the term "reciprocity" refers to exchange among entities operating within a larger whole that has the effect of improving the vitality of each participating entity, as well as the vitality of the larger whole. As a phenomenon, wholeness in a system depends on the number and quality of healthy connections among the smaller wholes or subsystems that make it up. It also depends on the integrity of those smaller wholes. For example, a person has to be whole within herself if she is to connect and contribute to the larger systems that surround her. Reciprocity occurs when each smaller whole nourishes the larger whole and is itself nourished by the larger whole.

As a manifestation of the archetype of the Hunter, the reciprocity entrepreneur pays particular attention to both the physical and the spiritual health of the community as a whole, and this often leads her to play a role in support of education. Reciprocity entrepreneurs are particularly interested in engaging stakeholders as critical actors with regard to integrating the contributions of business with the overall purposes of society. They seek to make their businesses so valuable and valued that they become nondisplaceable in the lives of communities and nations.

Reciprocity entrepreneurs are motivated to:

• *Create cultures of inclusion and interdependence.* The Hunter seeks mutuality and reciprocity in all relationships. When the tribe over-hunts the forest, the result is starvation. When the tribe turns its back on its members, the result is schism or war. The Hunter strives to keep the tribe whole and well nourished so that it can pursue its destiny.

• *Use setbacks as fuel for growth and development.* One can see the Hunter archetype at work in the almost awe-inspiring capacity of reciprocity entrepreneurs to translate adversity into uplifting accomplishment. The Hunter, in other words, knows how to take nourishment from everything life brings her.

• *Magnify the reach and the significance of every endeavor.* Because of its emphasis on wholeness, the Hunter archetype is particularly attuned to the way that even a small action, intelligently and strategically undertaken, can have a major effect on its context.

For Oprah Winfrey, prosperity comes from bringing everything into the light and everyone into the circle of humanity. Only then can humans be completely whole—included and interdependent—with each person living her best life. For years, Oprah has used the glare and public exposure of TV spotlights to help individuals shake off personal history and cultural assumptions that prevented them from being whole. In the process she has helped us all become aware of the unconscious assumptions in our culture that need to change. This makes her an exemplar of the reciprocity entrepreneur.

Oprah Inspired Me During a Major Life Transition

I had a personal experience of the positive impact of Oprah in June of 1992, when she cohosted the fifth annual Essence Awards, a program that acknowledges African-American women whose achievements have been mostly ignored by the mainstream media. I had turned on the television to distract myself. Little by little the ceremony drew me in, as Oprah described the challenges that each of these women had overcome. They had all faced poverty, most of them some form of abuse, and all of them significant struggles to rise in their field. Eventually Oprah told a piece of her own story, including the fact that she had been raped and molested by family members from the age of nine to thirteen. Until just a few months before this awards ceremony, she had blamed herself for that trauma. Then one day she said out loud to herself for the first time, "I am not responsible for my abuse."

This had a profound and cathartic effect on me, for as a young girl I had lived with an emotionally abusive father. Hearing Oprah say she was not responsible for her abuse freed something in me. She had asked me to experience myself as whole and complete, just as I was. For the first time, I felt able to take responsibility for my own future. Having grown up white in the racist South, I was unprepared for how inspired I was by this black woman and the powerful way that she represented what women could be.

Oprah's Rallying Cry: Turn Every Wound Into Wisdom

Oprah learned to translate adversity into accomplishment the hard way. For the first six years of life, she was cared for by a doting grandmother.

When her grandmother became gravely ill, she returned to the home of her mother, where she spent seven years living in conditions of almost unbearable abuse. At thirteen, she woke up one morning no longer willing to tolerate her situation, and she ran away from home. After a few months in the Milwaukee juvenile justice system—having been forced to return to her mother, then running away again—her absent father and his wife agreed to take her into their home in Nashville. She credits her father and stepmother with saving her life. Although her father was a strict disciplinarian (he demanded that she read a book and write a book report every week), he taught her the value of education and knowledge. He was striving to instill in her a sense that she should make the best of her life and accept from herself nothing less than the best that she was capable of.

Under her father's tutelage, Oprah began to thrive. She received awards for academic excellence, drama, and speech and was voted most popular in her high school. By the age of seventeen, she had the confidence to enter and win the Miss Black Tennessee beauty pageant. This led to a job at a local radio station that served African-Americans in the Nashville region, along with a scholarship to Tennessee State University.

Oprah had gone from being "broken" to being whole. In a short period of time she was able to replace and repair the myriad losses of her early life. Something had been stolen from her, yet she had figured out how to give it back to herself. When she was very young her grandmother taught her to read, particularly to read and recite the Bible and poetry at church. She was taught that her job in every part of her life was to be a reflection of God. She was to judge how whole she was as a human being by how much she radiated the love of God when she recited. Her grandmother told her that she was the face of God to other people and that in every person was the potential for God to have a voice. Even as a small child she knew that her actions could be deeply significant. She carried this with her through the seven dark years in Milwaukee, fanning it to life again as a teenager living with her father.

After two years studying speech, communication, and performing arts, Oprah left college and signed up with the local television station as a reporter and anchor. Soon she was hired away by a Baltimore station and then by a struggling Chicago-based morning talk show. Within months she had moved it from the lowest to the highest ratings. She realized early on that she had a calling to help others experience the same reconnection to self that she had undergone. But working inside someone else's rules severely limited her ability to pursue that calling. On the advice of movie critic Roger Ebert, Oprah launched her entrepreneurial career by renaming and then syndicating her talk show. Within a year this enabled her to purchase all rights to the show and to control its production and content.

Build a Media Platform That Makes a Better World Apparent

Immediately after the 1992 Essence Awards speech, Oprah redesigned and relaunched the *Oprah Winfrey Show*. She transformed its orientation from confessional (based on a belief that revealing one's most horrible stories can heal), to finding and claiming stories of inspiration that can make people whole again. The new show focused on literature, self-improvement, and spirituality—renewing her grandmother's message that God is potentially alive in every person. Although her self-help ideas were controversial in some circles, Oprah was determined to return to people their ability to raise themselves up to their full potential. In one interview she stated that she saw her life as an instrument for the human potential movement.

As an opinion leader with a deep commitment to a more inclusive culture, Oprah focused on serving marginalized people, parlaying her large audience and high approval rating into broader social understanding and acceptance. In February 1997, she played a therapist on *Ellen*, in the episode in which Ellen DeGeneres came out to the world as a lesbian. Oprah wanted to use her audience of twenty-two million viewers to change the American conversation about gender, sexual norms, and stereotypes. Through her show she introduced global audiences to a broad range of gay men and lesbians—celebrities, young people, politicians, public servants, military servicemen and women—people both ordinary and exceptional. She wanted, she said, to blur the lines between what was considered natural and what was considered deviant, and to make culturally acceptable what had not been.

Oprah's large staff sought out stories of transformed lives that could give hope and instruction to others who wanted to live up to their own full potential. She also promoted education, having had direct experience of its importance in her life. She created an influential book club and launched a program to celebrate people who found ways to transform a problem in their community. Her reality shows were about having everyone win, never about one winner.

In 2004, Oprah dedicated herself to raising money and awareness for the plight of orphaned, HIV-infected, and poverty-stricken children in South Africa. Her visits to the country led her to realize that young black girls were particularly vulnerable to the doubly destructive influences of racism and sexism. She invested $40 million of her own money to establish the Oprah Winfrey Leadership Academy for Girls, south of Johannesburg.

The academy uses various methods to cultivate a next generation of leaders. Girls practice self-governance within the school and are provided with superior academic training. In addition, they are given personal mentoring and coaching. Oprah says that she wants girls to learn early what she got only later in life: that they are fine exactly as they are and can make a difference in the world.

Help Them Hear What They Haven't Been Ready to Hear

Oprah took a wide range of social issues, from disability to race to war, and demanded an open conversation at a time when the mainstream media was too timid to address them directly. Every year, according to the Gallup Influence Index, Oprah has received high and favorable ratings—often as high as 74 percent and never less than 66 percent. This is not necessarily because everyone agrees with her, but because they respect her authenticity and determination to bring into the light that which is hidden and therefore divides us. Oprah has created an entertainment empire by scouring the planet for stories that will inspire and uplift people. She has done all of this entrepreneurially, becoming the first (and still the only) black female billionaire. On every entrepreneurial survey, she is listed as one of history's top fifty entrepreneurs.

As a reciprocity entrepreneur, Oprah has sought out stories from people who are cultural outliers. By presenting them as wholly human on her show, by helping them share their struggles and potential for rebirth, she has shown not only what is possible for each of us individually, but what it would mean to make an inclusive culture. This has come from Oprah's own hard-won affirmation of herself as acceptable in a world (and family) that had defined her as an outsider. She has openly shared her own fight to be a whole human being, and as a result, the majority of Americans are able to identify with her and the causes she champions. She has challenged and changed cultural assumptions about women, race, sexual orientation, education, and body image, building a sense of camaraderie across boundaries that have long divided us.

6

Larry Page and the Role of the Regenerative Entrepreneur

If you're changing the world, you're working on important things.
You're excited to get up in the morning.
—LARRY PAGE

Regenerative entrepreneurs are driven to break apart systems and structures that limit the full expression of potential. Men and women who take up this archetype see nothing as fixed and nothing as impossible. For them, everything can be transformed if one can find the right place to intervene. They look for "wormholes" that bypass the normal constraints of time and space, enabling change to occur rapidly. Such leaders are rare, and when they show up in society, people tend to talk about them as having marked the beginning of a new era. As a manifestation of the Headman archetype, the regenerative entrepreneur rallies the nation around living up to a higher expression of its inherent potential.

Regenerative entrepreneurs are motivated to:

- *Reinvent the world through vivifying first principles.* Like the Warrior archetype, the Headman archetype works on essence, but its focus is on the essence of governing institutions and agreements rather than products. By making the essence of the laws and agreements that structure civil society more vivid, a Headman helps people see the way to "a more perfect Union."

- *Use institutional jujitsu to evolve the benefits that our infrastructures deliver.* A Headman uses the weight and inertia of an institutional infrastructure (for example, the infrastructure built up around corporate law) to transform its use so that it can more beneficially perform its role or follow its mission.

- *Achieve the impossible.* The Headman archetype is particularly associated with visionaries. A Headman tends to think big and play a long game. It's this long view that allows him to make decisive, strategic moves that can, against all odds, transform the underpinnings of society.

Regenerative Entrepreneurship and the Founding of Google

People rarely think of Google, and its cofounder Larry Page, as exemplars of corporate responsibility. Yet Page has been using his platform at Google to foster major changes in our national and global business infrastructure, changes that indicate a possible future for responsible entrepreneurial practice.

From the beginning, Google pursued a radical, impossible vision, that everyone should have unlimited access to the world's information. Page believed that if knowledge equals power, unlimited access to knowledge would mean a profound redistribution of power. The transformation of information infrastructure is in the DNA of the company.

Work on Governing Infrastructure to Produce Big Change

Page's commitment to changing fundamental infrastructure can also be seen in Google's initial public offering. When Google went public in August 2004, Page sought to influence how ownership of public assets was regulated and how companies could go public more responsibly. The system for IPOs is designed to create stability in the price structure of a new stock. But it favors wealthy investors while failing to actually reflect market value and the workings of a free market.

This is because IPO's are generally managed by financial institutions that (1) have expertise in setting a realistic price, (2) can negotiate the legal and technical challenges, and (3) can maintain connections with other investment banks to ensure pre-public sales that demonstrate the validity of the price. In addition, the investment bank agrees to buy any unsold shares. However, in exchange for taking on this risk, the investment bank negotiates a relatively low floor price, with the intention of high profits on the upside. This arrangement more closely reflects nineteenth-century mercantilism than capitalism.

Under the leadership of its founders and Eric Schmidt (CEO from 2001 to 2011), Google performed a bit of jujitsu by offering what is known as a Dutch auction. Bidding was open to the public from the outset, and anyone could bid for a share. The investor set the price. Once all of the bids were in, shares were sold at the rate bid. The shareholder, not the investment bank, decided the price of the stock. This approach brought directness and transparency into the IPO, causing it to operate in an open market. There were no middlemen to be paid. It was a form of unadulterated capitalism that benefited investors directly and created a responsible market model for investing.

Even at this stage in the company's history, it was becoming clear that Larry Page believed that capitalism could be regenerated. It could be a powerful force for universal wealth creation, if its underlying essence and potential were better understood and if the infrastructure for managing it were better designed. Page's actions suggested that he was interested in transforming governmental, regulatory, and enterprise systems in order to manifest that vision. By ignoring the traditional IPO path, Google took on its own risk and made the sale of stock more democratic. The open IPO model calls everyone into the game, regardless of position, power, or wealth, and makes it possible for even small players to participate.

Five years later, Page took on the Federal Communications Commission. Initially, he approached the FCC about the auction of frequencies that were being converted from analog to digital. The sale was structured in a way that almost ensured that existing providers would buy all of the frequencies, because they were being sold in packages too rich for small players. Even though Google was not a bidder, Page decided to take on the cause because of its potential impacts on Google customers.

I described this effort in my book, *The Responsible Business:*

> As it is now, a wireless customer cannot participate directly in the use of bandwidth but can only access it though someone who licenses and controls use. You have to contract with a carrier to play, and use their wireless or cable frequencies. But customers want to buy phones and go where they want without restrictions. Google could see this. So they announced to the FCC that they were willing to bid at a higher rate to set a higher minimum, which could greatly accelerate the bidding, thus serving the FCC's mandate to return value to taxpayers. To do this they required that the FCC change the rules for how bandwidth can be used, and to ask for legislation to that effect. This new rule would offer a spectrum of bandwidth within which wireless service customers could go anywhere. Google succeeded in getting the FCC to change the rule for part of the bandwidth, even though they did not win the auction. They are credited with single-handedly setting FCC regulations in a new direction, knowing there would be no innovation without it. The taxpayer as an investor won, the consumer won.[1]

Beginning in the summer of 2012, during Page's second tenure as CEO, Google took on another high-profile cause when it began to question the effect of software patent wars on innovation and consumers. Pablo Chavez, the company's public policy director, suggested it might be time to ditch software patents. He cited Twitter's commitment to not block its rival's innovations through patent protection lawsuits. He reported that Google is now working on longer-term solutions that it believes will be healthier for business and society.

Regenerative Entrepreneurs Are Shaped by Up Close and Personal Events

To understand Google's orientation toward creating global change, it's help-ful to know a bit about four influences that helped shape Larry Page's world view: his grandfather's history in the early labor movement, his education in Montessori schools, his admiration for the visionary inventor Nikola Tesla, and his participation in the LeaderShape Institute when he was enrolled at the University of Michigan's engineering school. These helped build in Page the desire and confidence to take on large-scale systemic change.

In the 1920s and '30s, Page's paternal grandfather worked as a pipe fitter at a Chevrolet plant in Flint, Michigan. Prior to 1937, serious injury on the General Motors assembly line was a normal part of daily life for workers, and they could be fired at the drop of a hat for exhibiting a "questioning attitude." Workers could be beaten by their bosses. No gov-ernment organization ensured worker safety. No union negotiated for decent working conditions and fair wages.

As early organizers for the United Automobile Workers union, Page's grandfather and his peers risked their lives to change conditions for American workers. They locked themselves into the factory for months to prevent work. They fought and lost and then fought and won in the courts for their right to organize. Their efforts helped bring millions into the middle class and shaped a new ethic in America.

Page told Adam Lashinsky in an interview for *Fortune* magazine that the hardships of his grandfather's story made him want to make Google an entirely different kind of workplace, one that, instead of crushing the dreams of workers, encouraged their pursuit:

> My grandfather was an autoworker, and I have a weapon he
> manufactured to protect himself from the company that he would
> carry to work. It's a big iron pipe with a hunk of lead on the head.
> I think about how far we've come as companies from those days,
> where workers had to protect themselves from the company. My
> job as a leader is to make sure everybody in the company has great
> opportunities, and that they feel they're having a meaningful impact

and are contributing to the good of society. As a world, we're doing a better job of that. My goal is for Google to lead, not follow.[2]

How We Are Educated Fuels How We Intervene in the World

An unconventional education was a second significant influence in Page's life. Like his Google cofounder, Sergey Brin, Page attended Montessori schools until he entered high school. They both cite the educational method of Maria Montessori as *the* major influence in how they designed Google's work systems.

The Montessori Method believes that it has a

"duty to undertake, in the school of the future, to *revolutionize the individual.*" Montessori's ultimate goal of education was to create individuals who could improve society and were unafraid to take on seemingly impossible tasks. In fact, Montessori spoke at length about education for peace. "Everything that concerns education assumes today an importance of a general kind, and must represent a protection and a practical aid to the development of man; that is to say, it must aim at improving the individual in order to improve society."[3]

Maria Montessori believed that the liberty of the child was of utmost importance. For her it was imperative that the school allow a child's activities to freely develop. Without this freedom, children could not grow the personal agency that would allow them to serve a social purpose as adults. Thus, Page's childhood education promoted independence. It encouraged students to grow at their own rate. They were allowed large chunks of uninterrupted time to work on projects they created themselves. Students were encouraged to take on small-scale but real-world challenges and to invent ways to solve them.

It's easy to see how Google's well-known policy of encouraging all engineers to dedicate 20 percent of work time to projects of personal interest grew directly out of this educational history. And why collaboration without supervision is core to Google's work culture. And why

Page repeatedly exhorts his colleagues to generate "10x returns" with regard to the social benefits they are striving to create. He is recreating the inspiring learning environment he had as a child, where the focus was on growing free people with the capacity to transform society.

One of Page's childhood heroes was the eccentric and brilliant Croatian inventor Nikola Tesla. Tesla's work laid the ground for everything from lasers to radios, fluorescent lightbulbs to remote controls. He pioneered electrical engineering and developed the alternating current system of electrical distribution.

Tesla's story caused the adolescent Page to dream of making important technological advances. But he also knew it was a cautionary tale, because Tesla died in poverty, the quintessential "mad scientist." Page deduced that Tesla died penniless because he lost control of his inventions, and it dawned on him that if he wanted to retain control of his own products and inventions, he would someday need to start his own company.

The last piece of Page's development as a regenerative entrepreneur fell into place in 1992, when he was a student at the University of Michigan. Page participated in a new program called LeaderShape, whose motto was: *Lead with Integrity. Disregard the Impossible. Do Something Extraordinary.* Participants were asked to imagine a world without poverty, racism, sexism, crime, and all the other barriers to realizing people's full potential. They were encouraged to make choices, take risks, and develop a vision for change corresponding to their passion. Page says he took the admonition to make a really big systemic change to heart. He started by wanting to change transportation. (Actually, he still does. Google is working on a driverless transportation system that Page conceived in 1993, when he won eleventh place in the World Solar Challenge.)

As a regenerative entrepreneur, Larry Page has scouted for leverage points that allow him to use his position to influence the way the game is structured at the highest level. He has used the rules to change the rules (institutional jujitsu), often before people have had a chance to perceive the implications of what he has set in motion. Whereas most people see laws or regulations as an impediment to change, Page sees them as leverage.

Part Three
Being the Change Requires a Transformative Framework

Each of the four kinds of responsible entrepreneur uses four dynamic processes that can be mapped on a framework known as a tetrad. I call these processes *pillars* because they hold up the platform from which a responsible entrepreneur pursues her calling. The underlying framework is the same for each role, although the specific content changes. Understanding all four archetypes and how successful entrepreneurs have used them to build their enterprises will enable you to create your own roadmap. As your own work evolves, you will be able to draw on the methods characteristic of each archetype, as appropriate.

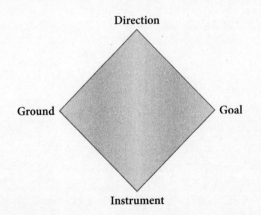

Figure P3.1 Generic Tetrad

The four pillars of the tetrad form a system; they are related and dynamically interactive, and you can work on them in any sequence. In the chapters that follow I have chosen a particular sequence that I believe will be most helpful to anyone trying to design their own unique entrepreneurial practice.

Pillar 1: Goal—the outcome to be pursued
Pillar 2: Ground—a foundation or starting point with real potential
Pillar 3: Direction—the guiding star that keeps a change effort
    connected to its larger purpose
Pillar 4: Instrument—the design criteria for a successful outcome

Because a responsible entrepreneur seeks to influence large-scale, complex systems, the work you do at each of these pillars will need to be deeper and more sophisticated than it would be were you simply trying to run a good business. Good business is simply the baseline from which to begin. What lies beyond the baseline is what makes the work of a responsible entrepreneur so exciting, rewarding, and meaningful.

Listen to interviews of Responsible Entrepreneurs who are *changing the world:* www.ResponsibleTrep.com/bookbonus.

7

Disrupting Industries
Four Pillars of the
Realization Entrepreneur

Life is not a problem to be solved, but a reality to be experienced.
—Søren Kierkegaard

A *realization entrepreneur* transforms an industry by renewing its purpose and values. The Warrior archetype, in its highest expression, defends not only the safety of a community and the integrity of its boundaries but also the values and aspirations that it strives to live up to. This archetypal Warrior exhibits more restraint and steady trustworthiness than aggression, but the sword or harsh word is always at hand if needed. Living up to the Warrior tradition requires inner development and strong courage.

In the same way, the realization entrepreneur requires inner development. The level of ambition to transform an industry takes a special kind of courage. Entrepreneurs are often thought of as risk-takers who need courage to overcome their own fear of failure. But I'm talking about a different kind of courage, something more like the courage of conviction. A realization entrepreneur cares deeply about the systemic evolution of an industry and has the courage not only to transform her industry but also to transform herself.

This work is different from product innovation, which, although it may improve a company's competitive position, only enables a company to play more effectively within the existing rules or belief systems of the industry. A realization entrepreneur goes to an entirely different level to access her insights—the level of the effect an industry has on its stakeholders' lives—and in the process she creates a whole new set of rules and a whole new order of industry.

The realization entrepreneur sets out to do something truly new, something that no one already knows how to do. This is where courage comes in, because the unavoidable apprehension arises: "There is no way I can look good at this." A realization entrepreneur has to give up looking good and being perfect. Her work is to perfect an industry; thus her sense of self has to expand. When you redefine the self to include an entire industry and all of its stakeholders, you sacrifice the ego-defined self as well as all the ways that you have come to define success, and this takes courage.

The Four Pillars of the Realization Entrepreneur

The following framework provides a systemic depiction of the characteristic dimensions of a realization entrepreneur's thinking and work (see Figure 7.1). I call the four points on this framework *pillars* because, taken together, they provide the necessary support for the platform from which higher-order work can be pursued. Each of the pillars is described in detail in what follows.

Pillar 1: Perfecting an Industry

The first thing that a realization entrepreneur transforms is her goals—from products that can compete in the market for a good return to products that align more perfectly the aspirations of customers and the success of all industry stakeholders. She works on *perfecting* the match between a product or service and its effect. As a goal this is more holistic than simple market position, because it looks beyond the product's use to what it makes possible that was not possible before. To be taken seriously

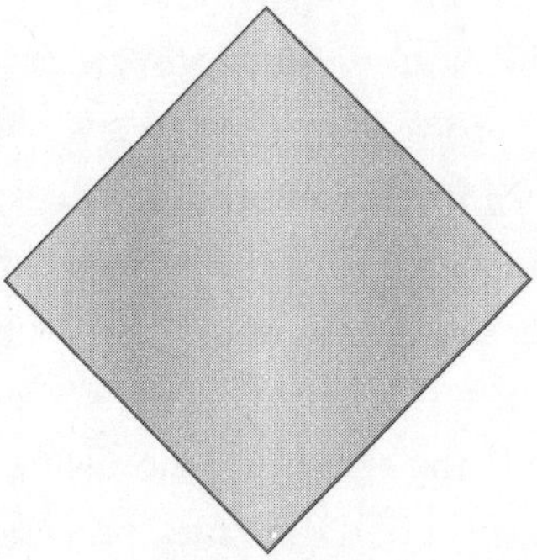

Direction:
Precision

Ground:
Integrity

Goal:
Perfecting

Instrument:
Full-Dress Inspection

Figure 7.1   Realization Tetrad

as an industry leader, a realization entrepreneur must be recognized for the high standards she achieves. Apple's focus on perfecting the effectiveness of its products established it as a leader in its industry, in the eyes of both customers and competitors.

In this context, realization is a principle-based obligation to pursue what is true, essential, and therefore better for all who are counting on an entrepreneur's creative manifestations. The goal of a realization entrepreneur is to achieve ever more perfect renderings on that obligation. For example, Jeff Bezos of Amazon says that his goal is to get closer and closer to delivering what consumers think of as the best possible shopping experience.

Perfecting offerings requires that entrepreneurs develop the capacity for envisioning products that enrich and empower their customers' lives. A realization entrepreneur must be able to run a movie in her mind of what it's like to live those lives. She must become expert in how her products integrate into their activities. She must make what her customers need before they know that they need it. Customers respond when they experience a business's ability to anticipate what they hadn't yet realized they wanted. They feel understood and cared about. This sends a message to the entire industry more quickly than any ad campaign can do and creates the best platform from which to become an industry spokesperson.

James Cameron, one of the world's most consistently successful film-makers, described this process in an interview with innovation expert Clay Christensen.[1] His entire filmmaking process—from scripting to filming to editing—is informed by the experience he envisions the viewer having. Even his camera shots are carefully constructed to enable viewers to project themselves into the world on the screen. He wants them to feel as though they are living the movie alongside its protagonists, and he subordinates every aspect of the creative process to this primary goal.

Pillar 2: Integrity Beyond Reproach

A realization entrepreneur must also upgrade the sources from which business actions originate. Most good entrepreneurs base their actions on a creative concept, something they believe people will want to buy. But if you want to change an industry, creativity alone won't be enough. You have to also base your actions on a commitment to *integrity* that is beyond reproach.

This is important because people will try to find your feet of clay. Although you will make mistakes, the more transparent you can be and the more willing to grow yourself, the less likely you are to undermine the trust and respect that is needed to fulfill the role of industry transformer.

Doug Conant, who led the turnaround of Campbell's Soup, maintains that integrity was his foundation. "Do what you say you're going to do. And do it well. How can people trust a leader who says one thing but does another?"[2] The responsible entrepreneur goes further. She challenges herself to live as though everything she does will become known, because sooner or later it probably will. Her choices are informed by an aware-ness of the effects that they will have on her company's credibility. Her Warrior's commitment to integrity beyond reproach prevents her from "accidentally" letting herself off the hook.

This is the antithesis of how many aspiring leaders were raised. They were taught to keep things close to the chest and not be caught making mistakes or failing to meet standards. But integrity beyond reproach is about setting your own standards—standards that are higher than anyone else's. It is also about allowing people to see your shortcomings as you work to overcome them and the growth that this enables. Courageous acts of self-development demonstrate not only the possibility but also the process of making a difference.

Pillar 3: Principled Precision

The work of the realization entrepreneur requires rigor and *precision*. When I work with business owners who aspire to be realization entrepreneurs, I help them maintain this precision with managing principles. These are intended to keep them on the path they've laid out. They provide direction and guidance for maintaining integrity while pursuing perfection. They also provide inspiration and renewed courage, offering a reminder of why the work is important and what its nature needs to be.

Managing principles provide a powerful alternative to standards, rules, and procedures, which in my experience produce at least two negative results. In the first place, they tend to narrow attention and thinking to the tasks and the results immediately at hand, when what is increasingly needed in this world is systemic understanding and thinking. In the second place, they are antidevelopmental. They define success and failure narrowly, on a task-by-task basis, and they fail to open up the space within which people can grow and learn and progress toward taking on more demanding objectives. There's no gradient built into rules, standards, and procedures. By contrast, managing principles invite improvement through time. Principles foster discernment as workers and citizens become increasingly precise in living them out. They are, after all, lifetime pursuits; one can get closer and closer to living up to them, but one never really arrives.

Here's an example of a principle from Jeffrey Hollender, founder of Seventh Generation: "Do work that is responsible and emerges from system thinking." A principle like this provides a stretch, something that we can get better at living up to. It calls forth our will, and in fact it is only when we choose to be guided by principles that will becomes a part of daily work and life.

Pillar 4: Full-Dress Inspection

By the time troops get to the parade ground, they should have already worked like crazy to have their shoes and buttons polished, their uniforms ironed and crisp. They know that if they have not paid attention to these details, everyone will see, and this evokes self-accountability. Full-dress inspection is about readiness to engage in a wider field of action—national defense in the case of the military, a marketplace in the case of a company.

In many cases, full-dress inspections are just for show, a display of power and threat. (Think of a totalitarian regime driving all of its tanks down the street of the capitol for the benefit of television cameras.) But when a realization entrepreneur adopts full-dress inspection, the intention is to get everyone to reflect on how well the company is prepared and whether it is able to be at the top of its game. The ritual of "calling someone on the carpet," on those occasions when it is required, is used to build collective consciousness about the need for impeccability from every member of the company.

This is one reason why it is imperative that full-dress inspection be done in public. The only appropriate place to carry out a consciousness-evoking dressing down is in a place where it can be instructive to all. However, this is rare in business; most calling on the carpet is done in private to protect people's feelings. That prevents the rigorous self-examination that a team or company needs do as a whole. The primary role of a realization entrepreneur is to establish a culture that demands the highest level of performance throughout the company and instills an appreciation for rigorous examination of thinking and results.

Of course, this means that everyone needs to learn how to not take dressing-downs personally. In companies with a realization entrepreneur culture, it is considered a sign of maturity to stand steady in a full-dress inspection, extracting learning from criticism but also feeling honored to be part of instructing and inspiring others. We admire as great leaders those entrepreneurs who know how to walk this fine line, who remember that a dressing-down is about consciousness-raising and not about humiliation.

I introduce this capacity into an organization through frameworks, which gives everyone an opportunity to share in the role of commanding officer. Frameworks make it possible to come to agreement about the inspection process before engaging in it. I have seen groups get much tougher on themselves when they had a framework as a basis for objective and rigorous evaluation. It actually takes personality out of the equation and places the focus on the work, which engages the will to get to the level of perfection that everyone aspires to.

Shadow: Insensitivity

Any archetype can be adopted in an unconscious or shadow way. In the case of the realization entrepreneur, this can manifest as insensitivity—the shadow aspect of the Warrior. Insensitivity is blindness to those around us. It affects the ability of a company to deliver on its promises. Insensitivity can cause us to fail to see the potential in a person and to experience him more as a thing than as a sentient being. People find it very hard to keep will and caring alive if they don't feel seen, understood, and valued.

Much has been written about this side of Steve Jobs, whose relentless confrontation made some people stronger but debilitated others. His blindness to his own shadow is often used as a way to discredit his adoption of the Warrior archetype. However, Jobs is certainly not the first entrepreneur, nor will he be the last, to be undermined by his shadow.

A responsible entrepreneur must work continually on her shadow, and this becomes much more powerful when it is an ongoing community activity of the business. It is important to be aware that the powerful benefit that an archetype can introduce into an organization can be diminished if the shadow is not managed. I use self-directed personal and performance improvement processes guided by personal aims to work on this in organizations. The purpose is to help people get better at managing themselves, so that they become increasingly able to take on big challenges. Regular time for practicing this work gets built into the company's routine. Everyone has the opportunity and encouragement to shift shadow from an unconscious force to a source of conscious growth.

8

Realization Entrepreneurs
Sarah Slaughter and Indigenous Designs

Reality is merely an illusion, albeit a very persistent one.
—ALBERT EINSTEIN

One of the greatest pleasures of writing this book was the opportunity to interview the friends, colleagues, and clients who feature here as responsible entrepreneur exemplars. Though their accomplishments are impressive, even daunting, they are humble to the point of self-effacement. None of them knew, when they began their careers, that they would eventually get to where they are now. As you read their stories, you will see that each started with only an intention and a rough roadmap. They refined as they went, taking cues from the changes they could see happening.

Responsible entrepreneurship is a learn-as-you-go proposition, and the challenges it presents are exactly what make it so rewarding. It's available to anyone with a spirit of inquiry and an aspiration to make a difference. The purpose of the detailed method outlined in these chapters is to make the work you are already doing more explicit, less intuitive, more focused, and less scattered.

A realization entrepreneur works on industry through a couple of characteristic core strategies. One is product substitution, when a new product is so widely adopted that it disrupts existing products. The other is filling an open niche, when a new product addresses an unmet need and creates new markets.

Sarah Slaughter: Changing the Building Industry and Academic Research Methods

Sarah Slaughter, a civil engineer and professor, cofounded the Sustainability Initiative at the Massachusetts Institute of Technology's Sloan School of Management. She is fiercely committed to holding businesses and governments accountable for the effects that they have on ordinary people. "Every human being has a right to life, liberty, and the pursuit of happiness," she declares, "and we need to be sure that the actions of our institutions actually promote people's health, wellbeing, and opportunity." This fundamental belief and her work as a sustainability researcher and faculty member have led her to become a respected thinker and reformer in a wide range of fields, from socially responsible business to disaster preparedness to green building and architecture.

In 2007, Slaughter worked with a group of MIT graduate students on a project in Vietnam for a Fortune 100 high-tech company that was locating a new manufacturing facility there. The company had asked them to identify the critical sustainability issues. It quickly became apparent to the team that virtually no one in the surrounding community had access to clean water, and that, in fact, local water resources presented an extreme health hazard to the population. The company had designed a self-contained water treatment plant that would provide clean water for workers and manufacturing processes, but simply cleaning up the water within the walls of the facility was a little like building a fortress that admitted a few and excluded most.

When the team presented its findings to management, the response was brief and curt: "That's not our problem." The students were taken aback (though Slaughter, with her many years of experience doing this sort of work, had known to expect it). For a moment, they wondered if they should narrow their focus in order to stay within the bounds defined by the company, hoping for the best later on. But because they were there as a research group and not as paid consultants, they chose to stick to their guns. This only escalated the conflict. The company began to talk about canceling MIT's participation in the project.

It was at this point that the real learning began. Slaughter encouraged her students to begin to develop scenarios around the systemic implications of climate change on Vietnam. They began to see connections between increasingly intense tropical storms, cross-contamination between sewage and an already unhealthy water supply, disease epidemics, and human suffering. It didn't take long to make the case that significant storm events would lead to a seriously compromised work force.

This time when they went back to present to the company, they got a very different response. The management reported that it had been profoundly affected by the team's ability to clearly illustrate the real human consequences of a changing world. They could see that by entering into this community, the company incurred responsibility for the wellbeing of workers. It was also obvious how untenable the fortress image was. What were they going to do in the event of a storm-generated emergency? Lock everyone out? Open the gates as a sanctuary and be completely unable to carry on with their work? It was lose-lose no matter how they looked at it.

On the positive side, Slaughter made the case that the company was already bringing in experts to address their own water system. For relatively little additional cost they could address the problem proactively by designing a clean water infrastructure for the region. They could easily afford to act as good corporate citizens and avoid the dire consequences of an almost inevitable disaster.

This little story beautifully illustrates Slaughter's approach to changing the sustainability research industry that she is part of. From her platform at MIT, she has overseen publication of many projects like this. People in her field have seen the value of her systemic method and quickly adopted the approach. She has been so influential, she points out with a laugh, that other institutions are now outcompeting her for project funding! She couldn't be happier.

In another research project earlier in her career, Slaughter set out to promote widespread adoption of green building technologies by demonstrating the need to change standards and procedures. One day she found herself standing on the end of an iron beam eighty-seven stories in the air over a Boston construction site. As she looked across at the steel worker attaching bolts at the other end of the beam, she suddenly realized that his perspective was completely different from the one she had been holding. It dawned on her that social and economic justice were as central to changing industry practices as the environmental and design questions she had been working on. She could see that this steel worker was never going to agree (nor should he!) to any change that might increase the threat to his life, and she realized that he was the key instrument for the transformation she sought to support.

Since that day, Slaughter has argued powerfully for engaging the intelligence and experience of workers and regulators in actively solving research problems that affect them. This has had a deep influence on the academic community of which she is a part, changing approaches and expectations about how research is done.

Pillar 1: Perfecting

Sarah Slaughter chose the field of research because she saw it as a leveraged way to help people understand the systemic implications of their actions. She brings a collaborative approach to a discipline that tends to work on things in silos; this approach stems in part from her multidisciplinary education as an economist, anthropologist, political scientist, and civil engineer. She addresses each research question from a systemic point of view and pays particular attention to the voices that are relevant to but usually not heard in connection to the topic (for example, those of natural systems and impoverished communities). In other words, Slaughter seeks to perfect the usefulness of her research by making it more reflective of the way the world actually works.

She set up her first company, MOCA, to work as a civil engineer with large-scale owners, developers, and builders, bringing a deep social consciousness to everything she did. She had by that time established a strong reputation for improving financial returns and was in great demand. She was consistently able to help companies improve their bottom lines through an unconventionally systemic approach that addressed such questions as how to increase worker health and safety.

Later, as a professor, she was asked by MIT to head an initiative that would work on energy efficiency. She said, "I'm happy to do that, but you can't actually understand energy efficiency if that's all you focus on." Energy, she pointed out, touches absolutely every aspect of our lives as modern people. In order to address it meaningfully, she would need to work across multiple levels of government, academic disciplines, and business interests. And, she reasoned, if she was going to go to the trouble to bring all of these people together anyway, they might as well work on other important issues where their expertise or jurisdictions overlapped.

The result was the Built Environment Coalition, which involves state and local governments, companies, academic leaders, influential non-profits, and key people in multiple federal agencies. These participants provide the input and support that allows the coalition to do systemic analysis. This is very important, because it greatly speeds up the decision-making process, resulting in public policies and investments that actually do what they were designed for.

What makes this remarkable is that, strictly through methods of innovative research, Slaughter has accomplished major changes in how governments and private entities develop or manage the built environment. She doesn't take on the role of advocate to create these changes—she doesn't need to. Her research is so effective that it educates and persuades as it is being done. Over and over Slaughter has been able to pull together players from across key agencies and organizations to work together on large questions that affect entire sectors of the economy. Because these people are active members of the research group, they are familiar with and invested in the information that gets developed. As a result, a systemic perspective becomes embedded in their thinking and decision making.

For example, recently Slaughter has helped federal, state, and local agencies and nonprofits understand the ways that climate change is likely to make regions more vulnerable to potential disasters. From this they have been able to build resiliency into key services such as hospitals, transportation and energy infrastructure, and food security. This ability to link systemic causes to diverse effects is characteristic of the research Slaughter does, and it is therefore becoming increasingly characteristic of the institutions she serves. Because her projects always include student interns, she is also having a profound impact on how the next generation of researchers will approach challenging questions in the future.

Pillar 2: Integrity

Slaughter has always scrupulously avoided any perception of conflict of interest. As her prominence and the scope of her responsibility have grown, her sense of personal integrity has required her to resign from the projects and organizations that she founded earlier in her career. More important, she has sought to use her position to push for a higher level of integrity in scientific and public discourse. She structures her projects in ways that enable her to maintain both the perception and the reality of objectivity. For example, in the Vietnam project described earlier, the fact that her team had volunteered to work with the company without payment meant that they were in a position to tell the truth, regardless of the company's reaction. In her role as a member of the advisory council of the National Academy of Sciences, she is able to call for a higher standard of systemic accountability from the scientific world.

Pillar 3: Principled Precision

One of Slaughter's most fundamental managing principles is, "When taking on a research subject, always extend your thinking to take into account the systems that affect it and those affected by it." Her very first research project was on the transportation system of Hartford, Connecticut, where she looked at commute times. She showed that it took two and a half hours a day for someone below the poverty line to get to work and back, whereas it took only half an hour for a professional. This gave the city's transit authority the evidence it needed to allocate part of its funding for creating a more equitable system. The resulting upgrades halved the commute time for poor people. When she is asked why she bothered to do this particular research, she says, "I wanted my students, many of whom were minorities, to understand how research could impact lives by impacting policy decisions."

On another project, she taught a course to explore the process of project management, using a specific site owned by a Boston developer. He assumed that the research would be focused solely on his project, which was to reclaim a Superfund site and convert it into a trucking transit facility. This would have brought a stream of fourteen-wheelers through the adjoining low-income neighborhoods, further impacting an already degraded landscape and quality of life.

Because the site was so contaminated, no one really expected much from this project. However, the team pulled together designers, architects, contractors, and construction managers and began to create scenarios based on extensive research—scenarios that went far beyond what the developer had been considering. Rather than limiting themselves to the site, they looked at multiple connections to larger systems: traffic patterns, community dynamics in the surrounding neighborhoods, the hydrological systems that the site was part of and contributing contaminants to, and interactions with local ecologies. They made very clear to the client the impacts that paving the site for a trucking center would have on all of these systems.

The concept that emerged from this analysis was a research and development center surrounded by a park. The center would provide high-paying jobs for local residents, improve the quality of life in neighboring communities (and raise their property values), and provide a keystone for further high-value development. The park would enable biological clean up of the soil and water while opening much needed green space in the neighborhood. This idea later became reality, and the area has undergone a complete transformation. The Superfund site has become a vibrant urban center with its own train stop, a living example of Slaughter's principle of extending thinking to take into account all affected systems.

Pillar 4: Full-Dress Inspection

In the Superfund project, Slaughter required her students to be front and center in presenting and defending every aspect of their research and the scenarios they developed from it. This was something they had never experienced before—defending research in a real-world situation—and they were met with a lot of skepticism and resistance from people whose credibility, livelihoods, and resources were at stake. These interactions were very much like the generals interrogating the troops, looking for any unpolished button or unshined shoe. The students still report that this experience greatly affected their later work by teaching them to be imperturbable. Sarah always puts the people who need to grow the most out in front, knowing that the tempering they will go through is vital to their becoming agents for real change.

Shadow: Insensitivity

Slaughter reports that she has a tendency to drop into the role of academic lecturer, which can become a real problem when she's trying to engage stakeholders in the field. It makes her insensitive, too Warrior-like, and it can alienate the people she wishes to reach. She has learned to see this coming, to take a breath, and to ask herself what principle or idea she wants to engage people around. Instead of launching into a lecture, she waits until she can find a question that will involve everyone in a developmental process to generate new thinking. Even when the stakes are high, she has faith that when she invokes higher-order principles, her students, colleagues, and stakeholders will rise to the occasion.

Indigenous Designs: Changing the Fashion and Textile Manufacturing Industries

When best friends Scott Leonard and Matt Reynolds were teenagers, they made a vow—along with a third friend, Mike Drapkin—that if any one of them got married, the others would come from wherever they were in the world to be groomsmen. Little did they know that this vow would launch the business that has defined their careers.

With the encouragement of a supportive mother, Leonard had learned very young that it is possible to take a good idea and act on it. By the time he was in third grade, he was organizing aluminum can collection drives to raise money for school lunches for low-income kids. After studying business in college, he worked for a while at a health food store in Palo Alto. One day, rushing down a city sidewalk, he accidentally collided with a stranger walking home, his arms laden with bags of groceries. Apologizing profusely, he helped the man up and collected his things off the street. The man, Joe Flood, and Leonard quickly established a friendship. Flood, an Ecuadoran, was passionately interested in the plight of his people, and their friendship awakened in Leonard a strong interest in this topic. Together they developed the idea of a textile company that would improve the economic independence of Ecuadoran women living in small villages.

Meanwhile, Matt Reynolds, who had also graduated from college with a business degree, had been hired by a retail company with a strong progressive bent, for which he was helping open new stores. When an opportunity to go on the road with his college rock band opened up, he got permission to take a leave of absence. Years later, he reported that this time on the road taught him what it means to be an entrepreneur, because the band had to find venues, promote themselves, handle logistics, and deliver a rousing show every night. Ultimately, though, neither retail nor rock 'n' roll really satisfied Reynolds, and he decided to spend a year traveling in Europe figuring out what he was going to do with his life. Halfway through his time there, he got the call to be groomsman at Mike Drapkin's wedding.

Of course, Leonard had gotten the same call. Sitting next to Reynolds at the rehearsal dinner, Leonard brought him up to speed on the Ecuadoran business. "This is what I've been looking for!" said Reynolds. As a child, he had lived in Latin America, and he was very conscious of the inequities that create poverty in the region. Within two days, Indigenous Designs took off, with Leonard and Reynolds providing guidance and energy and Flood providing connections to village knitters.

In the years since, Indigenous Designs has grown into a major supplier of organic and fair trade fashion produced in developing countries in Latin America. Its focus is on helping village women build strong businesses and communities. At the same time, the company has taken on one of the most polluting industries in the world in order to make it more sustainable. It has pioneered the use of organic fair-trade textiles and has become an important supplier for Eileen Fisher, a premier American clothing designer. Indigenous Designs is fundamentally driven to change how capitalism works so that its effects become systemically beneficial, and to pursue this aim by becoming excellent realization entrepreneurs.

Leonard and Reynolds's original insight was that "you can *perfect* the entire process of creating textiles, from sourcing the seeds to recycling the wastes, by thinking holographically about what supports a consumer's mental and emotional health." For example, wearing clothing made from cotton that has been heavily treated with pesticides or other toxic chemicals can harm the health of the consumer. Pesticides and chemicals can also harm cotton growers and ecosystems, and this can make consumers feel as if their lifestyles are at odds with nature. This disharmony diminishes the consumer's sense of integrity and self-worth. Indigenous Designs set out to correct this problem by perfecting the textile process, using the customer as an indicator for what creates health.

One of the company's stated principles is that "design is about being." People say something about who they are through what they wear, and for this reason Leonard and Reynolds are committed to ensuring that women who choose Indigenous Designs clothing know that they can do so with confidence. The company's aesthetic eschews trendiness and speaks instead to an understanding of beauty that includes such values as timelessness, compassion, integrity, and caring for a better world. In order for these values to be embedded in clothing, they must also be embedded in every aspect of textile production—another example of *perfecting*.

Indigenous Designs maintains a strong sense of *integrity* through a slow and very deliberate cultivation of relationships among key partners. When Leonard and Reynolds contract with producers, they seek out people with whom they share fair-trade values in order to build long-term and trustworthy relationships. Before they sign contracts, they engage in conversations to build and clarify these shared values and establish the basis for maintaining them over time. This same approach is extended to recruiting investors and even to establishing their clientele among clothing designers. They want to be sure that nothing they commit to in a business relationship has the potential to undermine their integrity with regard to core values. This emphasis on long-term relationships shows up even among the employees of Indigenous Designs, many of whom have known one another for decades.

Indigenous Designs' *principled precision* shows up in its premise that when capitalism is uncontaminated, it always produces equity. Conversely, when capitalism fails to produce equity for every participant in the system, the resource base is eroded and economic exchange becomes increasingly difficult. From this premise, Indigenous Designs has articulated the principle, "Build sustainable business capability in order to promote equity with our partners, so that they can generate opportunities." This has led the company to work with indigenous women, teaching them how to be successful small business owners, helping them create co-ops, and then helping these co-ops come together as an integrated system to ensure reliable quality and timely supply of products. As a result, village women have built the precision and consistency needed to participate and compete in a marketplace dominated by first-world businesses. They are able not only to maintain a steady working relationship with Indigenous Designs but also to organize themselves to find and serve other customers.

Full-dress inspection is precisely why Indigenous Designs opted to become a business rather than a nonprofit. Leonard and Reynolds point out that being in business makes you immediately accountable for your actions and choices. The market gives you pretty direct confirmation as to whether or not you are living up to the standards you have articulated. To keep its feet to the fire, the company has always maintained complete transparency about its operations.

Over time, Leonard and Reynolds observed that there were a lot of companies in their industry that were making false claims about sustainability and fair-trade practices. This was beginning to create a climate of mistrust among consumers. So Indigenous Designs supported the establishment of two different associations to create third-party validation of such claims.

The first is the Eco-Index, which assesses industries with regard to their impact on the environment. Eco-Index has compiled a very large database to track the impact of multiple industries on climate change and ecosystem health. The second association is B-Lab, which has established a rigorous and regularly updated assessment process to enable companies to become certified as exemplars of beneficial capitalism. These two associations have transformed market dynamics by providing consumers with a basis for trusting the claims made by green companies and holding them accountable.

One thing I particularly admire about Indigenous Designs is summed up by something that Leonard and Reynolds told me when we met: "To be this kind of entrepreneur, one who believes that you can change industries, you have to be a little crazy. In order to do it, you have to get up every day and take your crazy pill, because there are so many days when it feels impossible. Our crazy pill was given to us by an indigenous elder, who told us that if we took one step at a time we would walk far. So we did."

That's what I mean when I say that the particular virtue of the realization entrepreneur is courage.

Build Your Roadmap: Ideas You Can Use to Lead Change for Your Industry

Start from your customer's life and aspirations. Perfect your offerings to make their dreams increasingly possible.

Create the platform to make your innovations the basis for shifting an industry.

Maintain integrity beyond reproach.

Grow the highest quality of decision making throughout your organization through cocreation of and alignment around managing principles.

Submit to a public and ongoing process for rigorous examination of the effects you create. Build capability to handle the perturbations this will cause.

Impact Investors: Visit www.ResponsibleTrep.com/downloads to download your free workbook to apply *The Responsible Entrepreneur* concepts to investing your funds, guiding owners in making a difference, and evolving the investment industry.

9

Upending Social Systems
Four Pillars of the Reconnection Entrepreneur

Don't believe everything you think.

Businesses use social systems, especially economic systems, to influence how society works—usually, though not always, for their own self-interest. Sometimes this influence can be extremely destructive. For example, one socially codified means for determining fair wages is the minimum wage. As a rule, businesses react powerfully and as a group whenever there is any mention of raising the mandatory minimum wage. They claim that this will undermine their ability to do business and produce severe economic consequences due to layoffs and reduced hours. The social effect has been the establishment of a permanent underclass of workers who can never generate enough income to adequately provide for their families.

Ironically, research has consistently shown that businesses that provide wages considered fair by workers experience not only solid returns but active worker participation. Reconnection entrepreneurs are willing to shift a key system driver governing income distribution by challenging the mythical dangers associated with raising the minimum wage and advocating for the systemic economic growth that arises from paying workers fairly. What they know is that their businesses will prosper in that kind of income distribution environment.

Jim Sinegal has actively campaigned for decent wages for workers. He founded Costco, one of America's largest big box retailers, with the vision of building a company that would actually be good for the nation's communities and economy. His business model depended on a stable, well-paid, and committed workforce, and he worked hard to ensure that he was growing careers for his employees, not just temporary jobs. Costco has done an extraordinary job of providing workers without college degrees a way to enter the middle class, filling a role once held by manufacturing. Through this commitment, the company has actively contributed to more stable communities, healthier families, and a basis for engaged citizenship. Further, his commitment has led Sinegal to advocate at local and national levels for a higher minimum wage for all workers, and to argue that this is necessary for a viable economy and democracy.

Costco's business model is based on the idea that hanging on to its employees gives the company the leverage it needs to manage overhead. Many high-volume retailers and fast-food franchisers expect high turnover and irresponsibility in their workforce. This arises from the assumption that workers are interchangeable—commodities, if you will. This leads these companies to drive wages as low as possible, and to create comprehensive procedures as a way of ensuring an adequate level of performance. Of course, these assumptions come at a significant cost. High turnover is expensive in terms of recruitment, training, and lost productivity. Treating people as though they can't manage themselves incurs higher management costs and can easily undermine motivation. Costco, by contrast, is able to attract and retain lifelong employees who are highly motivated and require minimal management. Treating its employees as loyal and independently intelligent beings is great for productivity and innovation.

The role of the reconnection entrepreneur goes beyond products and services that are intended to address current social issues. A reconnection entrepreneur is less interested in symptoms than in underlying causes. So, for example, he doesn't just seek to help disadvantaged kids get an education; he seeks to change the social system so that it no longer produces the disadvantage in the first place. He doesn't just make a smoke-free stove for people living in Sub-Saharan Africa; he works on changing the system that fosters inequity among nations and robs people of the ability to determine their own future. A reconnection entrepreneur gets outside of the issue and asks himself how far upstream he needs to go to make change at the systemic level.

The reconnection entrepreneur is descended from a time-honored legacy—the court jester. Like the court jester, he questions the orthodoxies codified in the many diverse arenas of social relationship. He upends the known and validated rules of social engagement and rank, and he must develop enough wit and flexibility to avoid being killed by the monarch he serves. His task is to make ugly truth both palatable and playful.

Deep caring is a primary characteristic of the reconnection entrepreneur. Such caring goes beyond compassion toward individuals currently trapped in systems that limit them. A reconnection entrepreneur understands that if the system isn't changed, future generations will continue to be trapped in the same ways. He connects the present with the future to make the future accessible and intelligible to us. This drives him to challenge and innovate with regard to those systems that prevent the development of people's full potential.

The Four Pillars of the Reconnection Entrepreneur

The reconnection entrepreneur's approach, like that of the realization entrepreneur, can be understood through a framework containing four pillars that he pursues in a systematic way (see Figure 9.1). Although this

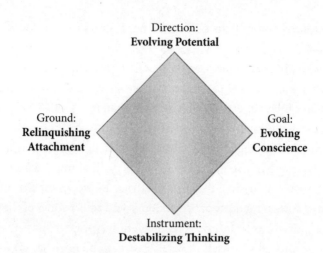

Figure 9.1 Reconnection Tetrad

process is intuitive or even unconscious for most reconnection entrepreneurs, the purpose of this analysis is to help make it deliberate and explicit.

Pillar 1: Evoking Conscience

Conscience is the natural or inherent human capacity to feel compassion and caring for others. It allows us to feel what others are feeling. This is a biological and psychological phenomenon, resulting from the action of mirror neurons, which allow us to produce a pattern of brain activity comparable to the neurological experience we are observing in someone else. In other words, "I feel your pain" can be an almost literally accurate statement.

It is possible to block the action of mirror neurons. When we choose not to engage with the suffering or joy of others, or habitually avoid emotional investment in the nightly news accounts of hunger or atrocities around the world, we disconnect from this neurologically based capacity. In modern times, this presents a difficult choice, because the flood of available information about the world's suffering is overwhelming and we lose our ability to make sense of it. So we all need to find appropriate ways to filter it or slow it down. The challenge is not to shut off our sense of human connection in the process.

The special gift of the Clown archetype is to help us walk this fine line. The Clown surveys the roiling spectacle of human society and extracts the key and essential phenomena that require our attention. This skill of honing and essentializing is what enables great comedians to shock us with the accuracy and pungency of their perceptions. The Clown uses this moment of shock and recognition to get us to see a way to something better. This enables us to stay present with what's going on around us and to focus on where we should be taking action.

A reconnection entrepreneur uses Clown strategies to get our mirror neurons firing and to get us meaningfully connected to the people and world around us. Whether he's working on connecting to his customers or enabling customers to live up to their values, he always seeks to help us stay in contact with our conscience.

To do this, he needs to take on the Sisyphean task of challenging and changing what most people believe is right, good, natural, or universally true. This is slow work, because no matter how often you evoke new awareness in people, their tendency is to slip back into old patterns of behavior and belief. You have to begin again the next day, usually with the same people, sometimes over decades or generations, working incrementally to change these embedded ways of seeing the world. Think of America's history with civil rights movements. Every change in law or practice was preceded by generations of slow, often unsung, sometimes dangerous effort.

How does a business reconcile the tension between challenging fixed ideas and producing personal and collective livelihood? It does so by evoking conscience in everyone, not only the already converted. This requires striking the right balance between introducing new thinking and respecting legacies that have been seen as a source of stability. The reconnection entrepreneur must cultivate the virtue of relentless caring, because this is what will sustain him and give him the tenacity to work in this arena. The reconnection entrepreneur also needs to be courageous about the values he holds and the condemnation he may encounter. Though others may judge him, he cannot judge them without losing his effectiveness as a change agent. Occupying the high ground requires caring for the evolution of values in society as a whole and caring for absolutely every member of society.

Pillar 2: Relinquishing Attachment

Attachment is the hidden enemy that undermines the development of human potential and the working of human systems. There is an extraordinary amount of research pointing to why we don't change our minds, even when confronted with strong evidence that an opinion or belief is wrong.[1]

This is not a new phenomenon. The Buddha taught that attachment is the greatest barrier to the realization of individual and societal potential. At the social level, attachment is the assumptions and expectations that we are wedded to and that define our reality. Attachment blocks or inhibits creative flow and is particularly destructive when it insinuates itself into an effort or task that requires collaboration. To be truly creative, all parties have to be able to develop their own thinking and open their minds to ideas they have not considered. They also have to be able to present their own ideas in ways that enable the group to build something together. Assumptions act like a hermetically sealed vault that prevents movement in our own thinking, while robbing others of the opportunity to have their thinking influenced by us. This degrades conversations and polarizes positions, creating a lockdown on creativity.

Relinquish Attachment as an Innovation Practice. Learning to see and relinquish attachments requires disciplined practice. Although meditation can be very helpful with this (and I recommend exploring it), I am speaking here about a practice that is embedded in the everyday life of a business. Let me explain how that might work.

Every engagement or task can be understood as a flow through three phases: input, transform, outcome. For example, to prepare a dinner we bring in fresh food and transform it by cooking in order to create the output of a meal that pleases family or friends. As a basis for disciplined practice, each of these phases offers an opportunity to become mindful of and relinquish attachments.

Let's take these phases one at a time, beginning with *input*. We typically enter an engagement carrying a set of assumptions about how it will play out. For example, we may second-guess what other people will be thinking and expecting. We may have expectations about how things should proceed and where they will end. Thus before we've even begun we've limited the room for creativity.

The antidote to attachment with regard to input is self-awareness. Catching yourself building an attachment, becoming aware of it before it takes hold, prevents it from running the show. When people work together, any time creativity starts to drop or walls start to rise, there's a good chance that attachments are the culprit. Pause and ask, "What assumptions are we making and what expectations are we holding? Are they preventing us from moving forward?"

Many successful entrepreneurs reflect this long before walking into a meeting or picking up the phone. They know how important it is to soften their attachments before they engage. The most successful businesses build this into a shared internal culture. Everyone in a meeting or project team understands that their input is important, so long as they haven't tried to build an irrefutable case for it.

The second phase, *transform*, has to do with how we get from where we are now to what we believe will be best for all. In this phase a lot of attachment comes up about how things get done. We can tell we have an attachment if we seem to be talking at cross-purposes or we feel that the other person is working on things in the wrong way. The only way out of this common predicament is for all parties to agree explicitly about how they are going to work. In other words, designing the process and getting people to understand and agree to it is key to maintaining consciousness during the transform phase. Although this takes extra effort up front, it proactively addresses the resistance that can derail a meeting or project when people are holding competing beliefs about the best way to get things done.

Deleterious attachments can also arise in the third phase, *outcome*. One of the most exciting parts of a collaborative process is the potential it offers to realize something greater than any of the parties could have created on their own. By contrast, attachments to output tend to arise from self-serving agendas as particular parties advocate for what they want.

The practice for addressing this kind of attachment is to develop a deep connection to what the group's collective work is intended to serve and to the output it needs to produce. When we experience ourselves as part of a group with a relationship that we care about to a larger system or purpose, we are released from our personal agendas.

One way to describe this three-phase practice is that it makes explicit what had been mostly invisible. Research into neuropsychology is increasingly demonstrating that attachments lose their power when people take the time to reflect. Once recognized, attachments become easier to release. Although the average business is unlikely to take on this level of practice, the reconnection entrepreneur knows that it is a necessary part of his work.

Pillar 3: Evolving Potential

A reconnection entrepreneur takes direction from his understanding of how the system he wants to affect works when it is healthy. He uses this understanding as the pattern for what he wants to bring into existence. This is quite different from simply trying to arrest disorder in the system. Put another way, rather than fixing illness, a reconnection entrepreneur promotes higher expressions of health.

For example, in spite of the technological, distribution, and financial prowess of humanity at this time in history, hunger continues to be a serious problem all over the world. Although stopgap efforts to feed the hungry will be important and necessary as long as hunger persists, the reconnection entrepreneur takes aim at the systems that keep the problem in place. To do this, he must design a business to transform the purposes and dynamics of the existing food generation and distribution system so that its overall potential can be evolved.

The first time I heard Charlie Krone, a mentor of mine, describe the core process of the food system as having to do with "bonding," it seemed far-fetched to me. But when I looked at bonding at the chemical, biological, and social levels, it began to make sense. Chemically, food provides the mineral constituents of living systems. Biologically, it represents reciprocal exchange within complex networks of systems. Socially, it connects us to place, community, and the celebration of life as we gather to break bread. Taken together, these purposes reveal some of the potential inherent in the food system.

When reconnection entrepreneurs working on the food system connect people to bonding, they evoke conscience and emotional relatedness in all stakeholders. Their enterprises offer a more compelling experience, because bonding is present. Innovation based on core processes like bonding actualize a system's true potential.

Pillar 4: Destabilizing Thinking to Invite Reflections

The reconnection entrepreneur seeks to destabilize people's unconscious thought patterns and break their attachments. The insight this produces creates the possibility for new understanding and conscience. This is not conventional business practice, but it needs to be brought into companies as an intentional way of working. Destabilization snaps people out of their normal frames of reference and pretty much always produces discomfort. The gift of the Clown archetype is to make this discomfort compelling, inviting, and even fun.

Destabilization can be produced by humor or surprise. One successful method is to ask a question that seems to come out of left field and yet has been designed to get people to see what they've been working on in a new way. Another helpful method is to introduce a thinking framework that slows down responses and has no obvious answers, which opens the space for really provocative questions. The idea is to invite discovery rather than project old ideas into the future. This kind of conversation allows a group to discover and awaken its own conscience, which is far more effective and far less self-righteous than admonishing people about the right way to think and behave.

Integrate Destabilization: Jeffrey Hollender Makes It Part of Hiring

Here's a good example from Jeffrey Hollender, who used this approach when bringing new people onto his management team at Seventh Generation.

Usually hiring is about persuasion. "I'm a good employee." "We're a good place to work." This discourages authenticity. Most businesses are aware of this, and they use destabilizing strategies to get around the masks. These methods tend to be confrontational and exacerbate the defensiveness of interviewees and the judgmentalness of interviewers—the opposite of what is intended, which is real and mutual discovery. Skillful destabilization is exciting, moving, creative; it awakens authentic conscience.

What Hollender aimed for in his hiring process was to give the applicant an experience that would develop her self-awareness. At the same time, he would use the experience to become more deeply connected to what Seventh Generation was about. When the applicant made it through to an interview, Hollender would give her a framework designed to represent the essence of the company by evoking images of it at work in the world, the ennobling purpose it was pursuing, and the unique value that it would generate. Rather than explaining these three fundamental aspects, he would ask the interviewee to talk about what they meant to her. Only after he had given her space to explore their meaning did he share his own interpretation. Then he would invite her to "interrogate me about how well I live up to this" and ask her, "How would this show up in the role that you might play here?"

The use of a framework meant that Hollender and the applicant were engaged in discovery rather than evaluation. Hollender was able to experience whether and to what degree a candidate was likely to be a cocreator of a business direction rather than a "yes-woman." From the beginning, the entire process was designed to subvert the behaviors associated with a normal interview. Both parties had to manage their reactivity in an unpredictable exchange, just as they would need to working side by side.

The use of the framework also helped produce an experience of collegiality. Both parties were on the same side of the table, working together on the same challenge. No interviewee knew in advance that this was going to occur. To preclude typical job interview dynamics, Hollender would start by explaining what they were going to do and asking for help in designing how they were going to do it. The process was transparent and collaborative by design.

Move from Ameliorating Issues to Changing Systems

Too often, people try to address social issues by using Warrior energy rather than Clown energy. As necessary as it is in its proper arena, Warrior energy can be counterproductive when it comes to conscience, creating polarization rather than reconnection. The reconnection entrepreneur patterns his efforts on the subtler, more demanding art of the court jester. The realization entrepreneur is a thought leader; the reconnection entrepreneur is a thinking leader. The realization entrepreneur is an authority; the reconnection entrepreneur uses Socratic irony, posing intelligent questions to help others evolve their thinking and creativity. He refrains from affirming their rightness or wrongness, placing that authority with them.

The practice of irony with humility enables reconnection entrepreneurs to destabilize people in ways that they find enriching and enjoyable. The goal is to evoke conscience in those who have become comfortable with their values and choices, without being cruel or judgmental. The court jester and the standup comic use self-deprecation to mirror their audience's self-satisfaction. Making people laugh about their shortcomings releases tension and is powerful and effective. Engaging conscience, when practiced well, allows people to reflect on themselves without feeling accused or embarrassed.

Shadow: Projection or Hypersensitivity

The shadow of the reconnection entrepreneur consists of three potentially destructive tendencies: hypersensitivity to criticism, projection of shortcomings, and "satisficing," seeking to console ourselves for our deficiencies ("I did all I could.").

When Richard Branson left England, cutting all his ties there, he was accused in the press of tax avoidance. He slammed back, aggressively denying the charges. This little bit of thin-skinned sensitivity earned him a place on the list of "heroes with clay feet."[2] A reconnection entrepreneur is at his best when he remembers to reach for humor and playfulness in the face of criticism.

10

Reconnection Entrepreneurs
Cheryl Contee and Kipp Baratoff

We have to raise consciousness; the only way poets can change the world is to raise the consciousness of the general populace.
—LAWRENCE FERLINGHETTI

All around the world, business is in a period of ferment and innovation, as a new generation of entrepreneurs look for ways to use and evolve the tools of capitalism in order to achieve more equitable and humane societies. The reconnection entrepreneurs introduced here have chosen to pursue social change not from an advocacy model, but instead through the application of the Clown archetype to business ventures.

Cheryl Contee: Revealing Questions Can Change Social Systems

Cheryl Contee, cofounder of Attentive.ly, has never shied away from provocative questions. In the run-up to the 2008 election, she was invited to do a public interview with Speaker of the House Nancy Pelosi, at that time arguably the most powerful woman in American politics. As a young woman, Contee had founded Jack and Jill Politics (now called This Week in Blackness), an influential blog dedicated to articulating the impacts of social systems on the everyday lives of African-Americans. She provided a voice that until that time had been absent in the blogosphere. As an activist-journalist, she had been tapped to initiate a different kind of conversation between the Speaker of the House and progressives, especially in the black community. As she saw it, it was her role to shift the conversation off of stopgap measures intended to fix a continually proliferating list of problems faced by black Americans, and onto the underlying causes that create those problems.

As she stepped onto the stage at the NetRoots Nation studios in San Francisco, Contee's heart pounded. She had prepared a question that came from dialogues on her blog—a question she knew was fundamentally destabilizing, going to the heart of the institutional, but largely unconscious, racism that continues to plague American society. Contee pointed out: "Our criminal justice system treats cocaine users differently from crack users, though both drugs are derived from the same chemical substance. And further, there is racial profiling implicit in the law. Although it is written under the guise of making the streets safe, it makes it unsafe to be a person of color on the streets. When will we make the streets safe for everyone?"

The room was silent. Speaker Pelosi thought for several moments, and then said, "That is a really important issue. The bill to address it has been languishing. I agree it is an unfair practice. I can work in Congress to help change the disparity in sentencing and the social injustice that this causes—and make sure this bill gets a vote. I am committed to that."

Later, when I asked Contee what she had learned from this experience, she told me, "Although I've never gotten over being afraid when I ask these kinds of questions, I realize now how powerful an impact I can have if I care more about changing the system than about what people think of me. When I was preparing to meet with Speaker Pelosi, I kept reminding myself that this woman *wants* to help, and my job was to ask the question in a way that she could see the opportunity to do so."

As a result of this interview, federal legislation was passed to abolish the inequity of justice regarding black and white uses of cocaine. The Fair Sentencing Act significantly reduced the number of nonviolent first-time offenders being sent to federal prisons. In addition, many existing sentences were shortened or converted to community service, thus repopulating the ranks of male heads of households in black communities. Judges, who had chafed under the arbitrariness of mandatory sentencing, welcomed the change, and research showed that the legislation actually reduced recidivism. Meanwhile, low-income families and inner-city communities, which had absorbed most of the impacts of discriminatory sentencing, saw major benefits as breadwinners were able to return home.

Teach Everyone How to Expose Problems at Their Source

Since that time, Contee has gone on to start two more successful ventures: Fission Strategy, which organizes digital campaigns to mobilize large-scale social action on important issues, and Attentive.ly, which helps social benefit organizations personalize outreach to their networks. Contee uses these platforms to help worthy organizations learn how to do the same thing she does as a reconnection entrepreneur: evoke conscience within society as a whole. The result is social change organizations that are increasingly effective as they move upstream from problem solving to work on the sources of problems.

Fission Strategy worked with MomsRising, an organization dedicated to growing a family-friendly America. They were taking on a whole range of issues that disproportionately impact mothers, especially low-income mothers. Why, they wondered, are European countries so much more supportive of mothers and families than the United States is, and how can we shift that?

Contee helped the group recognize the strategic opportunity represented by health care reform. They could see that, rather than chipping away at an array of problems and issues one at a time, through health care reform they could have an influence on the system as a whole. The problem was that they were a young organization and hadn't yet built the platform they would need to play on the national stage.

With the support of Contee's company, MomsRising developed a strategy based on shifting from advocacy to evoking conscience. They created campaigns organized around special days (Mother's Day, Valentine's Day) to raise awareness of the importance of health care reform to mothers and families. Then they tapped key people on their email list, asking for commitments to help them launch a social media outreach effort. Every one of these key people responded to the call, and the result was a wildly successful campaign that reached over 650,000 relevant players in the health care reform debate. In a matter of weeks, MomsRising became a leading voice on behalf of women for reform and was able to mobilize its community to speak out strongly in favor of the legislation.

Pillar 1: Evoking Conscience

From very early on, Cheryl Contee has known that she needed to make her voice heard, because she has something very important to say about the corrosive effects of racism on our society. As a young child, she heard stories from her parents about her great-grandfather's life as a slave, stories that linked his personal choices to the life of the nation. He escaped from bondage specifically to join the Union army during the latter part of the Civil War, an unselfish act that enabled him to participate in fostering a new national conscience. In her own life, Contee feels the same call from her grandfather to take the risk to bring about the next level of change for a nation.

Contee left the financial safety and prestige of a corporate professional life to pursue this calling. She had noticed that the emerging blogosphere was dominated by the voices and biases of white males, voices that were often unconscious of the effect of their commentary on the overall political direction of the nation. She found herself talking back to her computer screen in a futile attempt to challenge the thinking she encountered, but she couldn't bring herself to post her responses on the comment pages.

Then one morning she woke up and realized that a different voice was called for. Because no one else seemed to be saying what needed to be said, it was going to have to be her. She founded the blog Jack and Jill Politics, which is often cited as among the first notable African-American blogs and one of very few by women. The theme that ran through her blog was cause-effect advocacy. Her intention was to highlight various positions that others advocated, give an unshrill description of the effects they would create, and provide alternative paths and outcomes based on common attitudes in her own culture.

Even with this conscious effort to lift up thinking rather than slam the ideas of others, and even though she wasn't using her own name but a pseudonym and avatar referencing the famous escaped slave Harriet Tubman, her family was terrified for her safety. Her brothers begged her to stop blogging because they feared that this was an invitation to violence in a world that doesn't value nonwhite contributions to the mainstream discourse. But Cheryl knew that if she wanted to move the conversation beyond stereotypes and spokesmen, people had to know there were relevant voices from the black and women's communities that needed to be heard.

The Jack and Jill Politics blog had a significant impact on the lead-up to each of Barack Obama's presidential elections and resulted in her invitation to be the interviewer of Nancy Pelosi before an audience of tens of thousands of people. Contee is known for the quiet question or comment that awakens conscience in even the most powerful. She causes her readers and listeners to see the incongruity in their own thinking that can lead to behaviors that harm or diminish their neighbors. But she avoids harangues; instead, she gently, directly, and powerfully invites people to see their own lack of integrity, which gives them a loving space in which to change their minds. This is what she did for Nancy Pelosi and has since done for thousands of other people touched by her blog and media technology businesses.

Pillar 2: Relinquishing Attachment

Cheryl Contee is such a gracious person in a creative conversation. I once had an opportunity to talk with her after I had witnessed her speech to a Social Venture Network conference. She had been invited to talk about how to create appropriate infrastructure to enable more young people of color to successfully launch entrepreneurial ventures. In addition to receiving a standing ovation from an almost entirely white audience, Contee was able to mobilize strong support and investment in a project that targeted aspiring but disadvantaged young entrepreneurs.

I asked her if she was aware of her ability to move beyond race, inspiring people to care about the causes that she believes are important. "What advice would you give a person who wanted to have that kind of outcome?"

Her response to this question can be understood in terms of the three phases of a task (input/transform/output) detailed in Chapter Nine: "You have to get outside of yourself and look at the entire situation, or else it's very hard to have another perspective."

I asked her to explain this more and maybe give an example. Speaking to the *input* aspect of an engagement, she said, "I have to prepare myself for a conversation. I need to know if I'm walking in with any unconscious agendas, and as much as possible I need to let go of them. This is a good thing to remind myself of even in the middle of the conversation, especially if I notice myself becoming defensive or argumentative."

With regard to the *output* aspect, she responded, "I think it's a pretty normal human tendency to get fixated on wanting a particular result. It helps me to ask myself what's going to make the most difference for everyone involved. Even though that may sound abstract, having to ruminate on it gets me out of my own history and makes space for something else to show up.

"Once I've done that," she continued, turning to the *transform* aspect, "I can look for ways to change how the conversation unfolds. Having taken time out to think about everyone else's perspective, I'm able to invite them to help me figure out how we should have the conversation. This gets me over my own attachments, but it also gets them over theirs! Even after the conversation is in full swing, I find it helpful to remind myself that this is something we are doing together."

Pillar 3: Evolving Potential

Contee is working on what's at the core of democracy. She believes that we need to have a participative system of governance, and that without it, representative democracy becomes hollow or even destructive. Worse, it can be bought. You can buy a representative, but you'll never be able to buy every vote of a fully engaged electorate.

Toward this end, she has founded three successful ventures, each of which has endeavored to evolve the potential of the democratic process. This Week in Blackness confronted how the media presented black people in the news and gave a voice to the aspirations and successes of the black community in America. Fission Strategies and Attentive.ly work across the political spectrum to assist groups working on social change, including some of the world's leading NGOs and foundations. They use technology to match caring people with organizations attempting to create systemic change, in both the nonprofit and the business world. This effort has renewed belief in the democratic process and strengthened core social phenomena, such as electoral participation, volunteerism, and community stewardship.

When I ask Contee how she measures success, she says she can see individuals and groups rediscovering their direction and bringing new creativity to how they work on change. Her business tracks the number of people who are joining in, talking about, and actively engaging on issues and campaigns that they support. As those numbers grow, she knows that she's drawing people out of isolation and into full participation in real change. She describes her work as "reinspiring the human spirit."

Pillar 4: Destabilizing Thinking

Contee's question to Nancy Pelosi was inherently destabilizing, and it was offered with the authenticity, good humor, humility, and pointedness characteristic of a great Clown. Her purpose was to remind everyone present that discriminatory practices are inconsistent with what they stand for as individuals and as humans. The interaction caused the Speaker of the House, along with thousands of audience members, to stop short, pausing to reflect on how inconsistent unfair sentencing was with her commitment to an egalitarian society. Less than a year later, Contee received a message from Nancy Pelosi, celebrating the fact that this awakening of conscience had borne fruit that day when President Obama signed the bill into law.

Shadow: Projection or Hypersensitivity

Contee has reported to me that she must make a special and intentional effort not to take personally the barrage of stuff that comes at her. She says she can relate to President Obama because black people tell her all the time that he's not doing all he should for his community, and she wonders whether they are thinking the same of her.

If she doesn't stay strongly connected to the larger purpose she is pursuing, she can succumb to self-doubt: "I'm too young, too inexperienced, too scared to be able to pull this off." To calm herself, she uses the mantra, "Well, whatever I do, it's better than nothing. Any action, no matter how small, can help move the world forward."

Kipp Baratoff: Uniting the Strange Bedfellows of Commerce and Conscience

Kipp Baratoff is the cofounder of Fishpeople, an Oregon company that enables consumers to access gourmet seafood entrees that have been sustainably harvested and made with high-quality, healthy ingredients. Fishpeople's goal is to create a new relationship—to *evoke conscience*—between human beings and the sea, one that is deeply appreciative, personal, and mutually beneficial. The company pursues this goal by establishing exceptionally high standards and then working with suppliers to meet them.

Like all reconnection entrepreneurs, Baratoff is working on the transformation of a social system, in this case the way economic growth and stability get created. He believes that the way we ordinarily try to build local economies doesn't work. The dominant model is to initiate development at the national policy level in Washington, DC, or through recruiting large companies into a community. Baratoff believes that economic development must start and end locally if it is to *evolve* any real *potential* and staying power.

In his work as a San Francisco–based financial analyst prior to moving to Portland, Baratoff had gained broad knowledge about a variety of sustainability-oriented economic issues and opportunities. So when he and his partner began to look at their options, they quickly realized that fishing along the Pacific Northwest coast was a deeply troubled industry with local leverage and national significance. He and his partner reasoned that if they could rebuild that industry around sourcing and processing fish locally into value-added products, as opposed to commodities, then the region's coastal communities could rebound. This would become a template for economic development in struggling fishing communities around the country.

As Baratoff reports, he has spent his adult life endeavoring to bring commerce and conscience into the same thought. Fishpeople has developed its culture around a set of values that explicitly endeavors to integrate commerce with conscience. These six values are priced right; convenient; high quality; sustains the oceans; healthy for consumers; and supports fishermen and farmers. They are deliberately introduced into conversations among employees and with suppliers, distributors, and customers. According to Baratoff, all six of these values must be incorporated into any decision or action having to do with the work of the company and its place in the world. Anyone at any level in the organization can bring work to a halt if they see that a value has been overlooked or violated. Fishpeople aims to do this so well, both financially and in terms of branding, that it grows large enough to positively impact practices throughout the supply chain.

Fishpeople recognizes that, if it is to evoke conscience at the organizational level, it has to function nonhierarchically, so that each individual can become wholly responsible for his or her own actions and the actions of the organization. This has required management to *relinquish* any *attachment* it might have had to dictating decisions or the allocation of resources. As Baratoff puts it, "People are people. They are not just job descriptions. A team needs to be fully engaged. They need to base their collaboration on shared values so they can make decisions that actually do integrate conscience and commerce. We have a bell on the table that we ring before every meeting to remind us to 'intentionally arrive' and get prepared to live up to our commitments."

Relinquishing attachment has been a core aspect of Baratoff's development as a leader. As a child, he suffered severe abuse. In addition, he had a cleft palate that disfigured his face, and he was tormented by his peers. He grew up struggling with questions of power and its uses and abuses. During his first entrepreneurial endeavor, he encountered a mentor who gave him a way to reframe these questions. That changed his life. As he describes it, "There are three distinct phases in our relationship with power that we can move through or not. The first phase is the accumulation of power. People can get stuck there for their entire lives. The second phase comes when you use that power. The third phase comes when you realize that you have the ability to give power away." It is at the level of "giving power away" that Baratoff has chosen to work as a leader in his organization. "Although imperfectly," he hastens to point out.

To distinguish its products, Fishpeople sets and fulfills very high standards. Normally in businesses like this, the company works one on one with suppliers to hold them accountable for meeting quality standards (or it goes and finds other suppliers who will). But that approach doesn't produce the desired result of bringing commerce and conscience together. Conscience requires free choice—and that, of course, can't be mandated.

Fishpeople organized all of the players from every part of the value-adding process to learn how they were connected and how they impacted everyone else in the stream of production. This has meant that Fishpeople's work can actually *evolve* new *potential* for all of the companies with which it does business. As it scales its consumer brand, it will create a powerful ripple effect on the seafood industry in its region. As a result, participating businesses will be able to proudly point to their accomplishments as exemplars of what is possible for fishing communities all around the country.

Destabilization is core to Baratoff's strategy, and he uses it intentionally within Fishpeople. The six primary values are constantly used to prevent anyone from going on automatic pilot. They are posted on every wall of the meeting room so that it's impossible to ignore them. Time is built into every meeting to *reflect* on how well they are being implemented. Like the jesters they are at heart, the Fishpeople team uses its own secret signal to call the question of whether it is in integrity with Fishpeople values. Anyone can make a "fish face," which cracks everyone up and reminds them to slow down to think something through more carefully or to treat each other more gently.

Destabilization gets extended into the world more generally through Fishpeople's practice of radical transparency. One of the company's innovations has been to adapt the Quick Response Code (the square digital pattern that allows smart phones to access information about a product or company) to enable any consumer to find out, on any given package of fish, everything they could possibly want to know about it: the GPS point where the fish was caught, the captain and the name of his boat, the plant where the fish was processed or packaged, all additional ingredients and where they were sourced, and test results from that specific fish for any chemical residues. Talk about creating accountability! The captain knows that his name shows up on that QR Code; so do the owner of the processing plant and the distributor. Not only does this reinforce people's pride of workmanship, but it also strengthens their sense of mutual responsibility. If any one part of the value-adding stream fails, the whole stream fails.

Radical transparency is helping Fishpeople influence the seafood market. It has enabled consumers to become more educated and discriminating buyers. It has put other seafood providers on notice. And it has powerfully engaged distributors, who want to be associated with brands that are recognized for their high integrity and authenticity. Transparency is rapidly becoming the standard for such brand acceptance, and Fishpeople is raising the bar on what transparency really means.

Build Your Roadmap: Ideas You Can Use to Lead Change for a Social System

Evoke conscience by creating full transparency about choices and their impacts.

Ask questions that call attention to invisible impacts. Be provocative.

Examine your unconscious attachments. What are you bringing in? What are your beliefs about the "right way" to do things and the "right outcomes" you expect?

See potential in everyone. Design growth and development into everything, for everyone.

Be fearless but caring about using destabilizing questions, humor, stories, and processes.

Embrace your hypersensitivity and develop visual cues to manage it.

Impact Investors: Visit www.ResponsibleTrep.com/downloads to download your free workbook to apply *The Responsible Entrepreneur* concepts to investing your funds, guiding owners in making a difference, and evolving the investment industry.

11

Shifting Paradigms and Beliefs
Four Pillars of the Reciprocity Entrepreneur

There's always a story. It's all stories, really. . . . Change the story, change the world.
—TERRY PRATCHETT, *A Hat Full of Sky*

Our world is changing rapidly, and this places enormous strains on cultures. To remain resilient and viable, cultures need to evolve their paradigms and beliefs. The challenge is that there are so few people who can rise above the professional or community world views in which they are steeped to discover and appreciate new or alternative paradigms with culture-evolving potential. This is the work of the Hunter archetype and of the reciprocity entrepreneur.

Within a business culture, this inability to work flexibly with multiple paradigms usually shows up as the belief that different stakeholders are fundamentally divided and that their interests are antagonistic. Trade-offs are the inevitable result when this belief holds sway. Businesses separate sustainability from customer service from human resources from community relations, and because the blindness is pervasive this feels like a completely normal and rational way to do business. The introduction of reciprocity into this equation calls for a role that can rise above and reknit the links. This reciprocity role is inherently challenging and requires committed self-development. People who can step into it are rare, because it calls for detaching from certainty about one's own interpretation of reality. But without it, a leader is likely to perpetuate the divisiveness of society, even within her own company.

Reciprocity Is About Wholes, Not Parts

The reciprocity entrepreneur asks, "What is good for the whole, through time, and not just for this moment or for this group?" Most people work on what they think is good but overlook other voices and different perspectives. This role tells the story from all of the different perspectives and mindsets.

Reciprocity is usually defined in terms of exchange of value, in which positive actions elicit positive responses, and negative actions elicit negative ones. But when conceived of systemically, reciprocity takes into account far more than the effect of a simple exchange, because action always happens within context and thus tends to create ripple effects, which set up resonances or dissonances at higher levels of system. Taking on the role of reciprocity entrepreneur means stepping into this complex web of relationships, actions, and consequences, and taking stewardship for the working of the cultures and belief systems that must be reconciled for the sake of the vitality and viability of the system as a whole.

Inability to experience reciprocity closes off pathways to gratitude, generosity, humility, aliveness, connectedness, and relatedness. When I can't appreciate something different from myself, I make myself partial. This makes me defensive and creates territorial divisions between what is me and what is not me; fixed beliefs are reinforced, and the potential for conflict escalates. The role of the reciprocity entrepreneur is to unstick the certainties and create space for an evolution in understanding—not only of others but also of ourselves.

The Reciprocity Archetype Role Carries Bigger Risks—And Rewards

Playing this archetypal role carries risks. People who thought you were on their team may experience you as a traitor, when all you are seeking is a larger peace. For example, when black leaders like Barack Obama or Oprah Winfrey begin to provide leadership for all races, they may be accused of betraying their own history. Certain capabilities gleaned from life experience need to be present in order to successfully utilize the Hunter archetype, including the ability to redefine self and what self means, to reframe the idea of "other," and to generate compelling alternatives to existing cultural worldviews.

The Hunter is the provisioner for her tribe. She goes out into a dangerous world to get what's needed for the health of the community. At its best, Hunting has two key dimensions. The first has to do with releasing ego in order to become one with the terrain and the movements and behaviors of animals. The second has to do with the discernment needed to nourish the tribe without depleting the larger living community that it depends on for future nourishment.

In the same way, the reciprocity entrepreneur illuminates the larger whole within which a business is embedded and seeks to integrate the multiple forces and elements that enable that whole to be mutually (reciprocally) nourishing. This includes knowing how to bring into a group whatever is outside of it that will support its health and continued evolution, even if what is needed is split off, alien, and feared.

The Reciprocity Entrepreneur Is a Discerning Storyteller

The reciprocity entrepreneur engages people with images and stories that both undermine and enlighten. This is one of the roles that entertainment and the arts play, because they allow us to try something on without having to necessarily agree with it. Storytelling has power in part because it invites us to immerse ourselves in an alternate interpretation of life and gently dislodges our worldviews in the process. Brain science has demonstrated that once our brain is given an opportunity to image something working, it becomes part of our reality.

Work on cultural paradigms or beliefs can create a deeper and more lasting impact than work on social systems. However, it is also much more challenging. A reciprocity entrepreneur has to approach her task indirectly. Rather than destabilize, her work is to erode unconscious assumptions over time. Many reciprocity entrepreneurs choose to be internal agents, using the resources and platforms provided by existing organizations to support their sustained efforts.

Discernment is the reciprocity entrepreneur's primary virtue. It expresses itself through two particular practices. The first is intentionality with regard to effects. A Hunter recognizes that she lives and works in a dynamic living context and that whatever she does will inevitably have an effect. By becoming intentional, she can make those effects more meaningful and positive. But this requires discernment, which is based on understanding how an action or choice will play out through time.

The second practice is to relate to people as developmental beings who are growing and changing throughout their lives. If she has the capacity for discernment, a Regenerative Entrepreneur can participate in the growth of individuals and groups in ways that take into account their stage of development at any given moment. She rethinks how to engage each person or group with every new interaction. This practice is one of the fundamental drivers of success in building community and stakeholders.

The Four Pillars of the Reciprocity Entrepreneur

Like the realization and reconnection entrepreneurs, the reciprocity entrepreneur is working on a complex system. In this case, the complexity is related to the internal and often unconscious beliefs that drive the way we construct our social arrangements. To do this work requires a method that is correspondingly whole and complex. The four pillars offer a dynamic and systemic way of thinking about this method (see Figure 11.1).

Figure 11.1   Reconnection Tetrad

Pillar 1: Wholeness

Wholeness is the overarching goal of the reciprocity entrepreneur. She is always cognizant of her own thinking, language, and imaging in order to ensure that the characteristic of wholeness shows up in her leadership and business actions.

This is always easier to do in a consistent and rigorous way when she has some way of structuring her thinking. There are five characteristics of any living whole. A reciprocity entrepreneur can use these characteristics to evoke the experience of wholeness in herself, her product offerings, and her interactions.

Five Characteristics of Wholeness

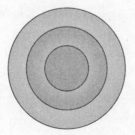

1. Wholes are **nested** within other wholes and are themselves nests for smaller wholes. By nested, I mean that these systems are related in a way that goes beyond mere connection to the *roles* that different levels of system play with regard to one another.

A familiar example will help to make this more concrete. A vibrant farmers market is nested within larger systems—a city and a region—and smaller systems are nested within it: vendors and shoppers. The organization that runs the market recognizes that it has a necessary role in facilitating the quality of experience and value of exchange for all who participate. At the same time, it understands that the market has a role to play as an economic engine and good citizen in its neighborhood, district, or community, and that ultimately it plays a critical role in sustaining and evolving a viable regional agriculture system and the cultural legacy that goes with it.

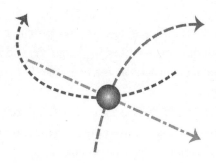

2. Every whole works as a **node**. This means that it has a multiplicity of energy streams or interactions that intersect in and around it. Reciprocity entrepreneurs look for those intersections and use them to leverage their efforts in order to influence the system as a whole.

Farmers markets have the potential to revitalize neighborhoods or neglected downtown areas. One way they do this is by attracting and stimulating exchange among extremely diverse constituencies. They are also able to coalesce the political support needed to take on larger, more intractable challenges, such as the loss of critical farmland. As a vibrant neighbor they shore up and strengthen local culture, pride, and sense of identity.

3. Every whole has a unique *essence* that defines it and without which it would not be itself. The reciprocity entrepreneur looks for essence in every person, every raw material, and every offering she makes. Essence awareness is good for a business because it avoids commoditizing people and products, but it is even better for natural systems because it avoids treating them as generic sources of extractable raw materials.

One reason that people love to visit farmers markets, especially if they are coming from out of town, is that markets give them a vivid sensual experience of a community's unique flavors, cuisine, arts, stories, and ways of interacting. This is also the reason why so many people are so deeply loyal to their farmers market. They know that they are doing the virtuous work of keeping the story or essence of their place alive.

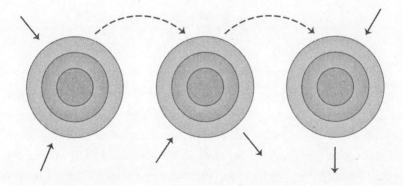

4. Wholes can be understood only by *imaging* them working, rather than by dissecting them into parts. The reciprocity entrepreneur must overcome her conditioning and let go of the analytical mind and the impulse to break wholes into parts and pieces. Rather than viewing life as snapshots in time, she must develop the capability to image systems

as whole, alive, and at work. Then she must develop this capability in her constituents. Stories and examples evoke the imaging capability that lies dormant in all of us. The reciprocity entrepreneur always strives to move people away from fixed ideas to moving images of alive, malleable systems seeking their own next possibility.

A farmers market can't really be understood through its parts—the vendors, the produce, the organizers and their jobs. One understands it by imaging it open and working, alive with transactions and exchanges, electric with creativity and the effort that goes into feeding people and making them happy. An image like this makes the market alive and dynamic for us.

5. A whole always serves a *purpose* with regard to the health and evolution of systems that it is nested in. All living systems have the innate potential to move to higher degrees of complexity, integrity, and reciprocity, the realization of which depends on the contribution of smaller systems. The contributions that move up and down through nested systems are what keep the world evolving and improving. Purpose is easiest to see in the lives of those systems that we call human beings. Each of us is born with an innate desire to learn, grow, and have beneficial effects on our families, communities, and ecosystems. For us, a meaningful and healthy life necessarily includes contributions to larger systems that help to make the whole world better for everyone.

To think about a farmers market in terms of its systemic purpose, one has to see it in relation to the larger systems it is nested in and the future challenges and opportunities facing those systems. For example, farmers markets are expressions of a larger movement to provide communities with locally grown foods. How a market participates in this movement has implications not only for economic development in its region but also for regeneration of healthy ecosystems. A farmers market that takes itself seriously will learn how to work on these challenges.

The Reciprocity Entrepreneur and Wholeness

An entrepreneur operating from the Hunter archetype maintains a comprehensive, consistent, and rigorous sense of wholeness. Traditionally businesses see their world as a "flatland," rather than a multidimensional living sphere. They work on products that they can sell, rather than effects that they can produce in greater and smaller systems. They take a fragmented approach and look at problems and parts, rather than seeking the nodes where strategic interventions can transform a system. They look at surfaces (such as current trends and what people say they want) rather than essence (such as what people are trying to manifest through their lives and don't yet know how to describe). They treat materials, processes, and people as if they were fixed or unchanging, rather than encouraging them to evolve to higher-order versions of themselves.

In his satiric allegory, *Flatland: A Romance of Many Dimensions*, Edwin Abbott imagines a two-dimensional world as a way to critique the ignorance that comes from too narrow a worldview. The book's protagonist, Square, is enchanted when he first encounters a third dimension, but he becomes frustrated when he is unable to persuade his fellow Flatlanders of its power and possibility. Like Square, reciprocity entrepreneurs see what others can't. But unlike him, they know that it takes time to become aware of new dimensions. They learn to be highly innovative because, in truth, they operate within systems that don't exist until they invent them.

Reciprocity entrepreneurs set out to make changes that are reciprocally nested in larger wholes that almost no one else can see. Their task is to make this wholeness self-evident by evoking living images that make it compelling and intelligible and to grow this new understanding into the larger culture through their businesses and offerings. This is how they bring nourishment to their communities and the world.

Pillar 2: Significance

To get up above the distractions and pressures of daily operations and see what really matters, a reciprocity entrepreneur has to shift scope. She has to step up one or two levels of system beyond what she would ordinarily be expected to consider her territory or responsibility. In my book *The Responsible Business*, I described one way to do this by using a framework I called the *stakeholder pentad*. The pentad illustrates the relationships among the five key stakeholders in any business and provides a way to think about:

a. The business's customers
b. How the business's cocreators, including employees and suppliers, can contribute to its customers' lives
c. How local ecosystems and Earth as a whole can benefit from better choices about the use of resources
d. How a business's work can support the communities it touches
e. How investors can get the enduring "virtuous" returns that they count on

Understanding that a business has a living context is the important first step to entering into a reciprocity frame of reference. The mistake most businesses make is to base their work on transactional relationships, asking only what they need from stakeholders and what they have to give in return. Systemic reciprocity is never merely transactional. In the world of the reciprocity entrepreneur, significance is defined from the perspective of stakeholders and what makes it possible for them to make contributions to larger wholes. Creating this image of interrelated stakeholders in the minds of the people internal to your business enables them to better comprehend systems and understand the meaning that their decisions will have for your stakeholders. They can then begin to see how they are contributing to significant change in the larger world simply by showing up at work every day.

You begin to show up in the world of the reciprocity entrepreneur when you let go of the idea that reciprocity is nothing more than a two-way street. It is actually a complex set of dynamic relationships among nested systems that nourish and evolve one another. You build reciprocity when you make choices based on what is significant at least two levels of system beyond the immediate effect of your actions.

Pillar 3: Destiny

It takes a strong sense of direction to stay on an aspirational path, particularly for the reciprocity entrepreneur, who tends to think big. She must anchor her work in the destiny of the living systems she wishes to serve. Destiny is defined as "the events that will *necessarily* happen to a particular person or thing in the future." A reciprocity entrepreneur seeks to understand how a system, if it is to remain true to itself, will necessarily behave and what it will necessarily become.

I call destiny, this inner necessity, a *global imperative*. Global imperatives are articulations of the right and proper working of something when it is operating and evolving as it was designed or created to do. Global imperatives are not negotiable, in the same way that breathing oxygen is not negotiable for a human body. They are a form of social or natural law. For example, "Democracy works only when it has an educated and engaged citizenry." This is a global imperative in the social arena (one that Seventh Generation used to guide its work), and it describes the destiny of democracy—if it is to truly remain democracy.

Global imperatives provide reference points, helping us understand how a thing really works before we intervene in it. For example, if we wish to change voting patterns, we need to understand the relationship between voting and democracy. If we were to buy votes, we'd be violating the social imperative just described. Because human beings can and should intervene in the flow of life, we need social and planetary imperatives. These provide the rigor that helps us contribute to the working of systems and processes in ways that benefit all of life.

It is important to remember that we generate imperatives, and also that they will be limited by the level and quality of our understanding. Imperatives serve as reference points, and as our understanding evolves, so can our articulation. They help us make wiser decisions, but even more important, they help us become wiser about our decision-making processes.

In my work with entrepreneurs and leaders I have observed great benefit accrue to those who take the time to articulate these master beliefs about how society and planetary processes thrive and prosper. They are able to imbue their businesses with these imperatives, giving them the capacity to move with sympathy, agility, and great creativity into reciprocally beneficial relationships with the world.

Pillar 4: Camaraderie

A reciprocity entrepreneur works to build camaraderie as her primary instrument for creating change within a system. This is because so much of her work is about overcoming the fragmentation that arises from the ways we put people into boxes and then shun them for not being like us. The societal impact of this exclusionary process is extremely costly to the individuals who are excluded and also to the camaraderie that binds us together as a society.

The best sports coaches in the world work with teams as reciprocity entrepreneurs (although their opportunities to create real beneficial change in the world are limited by the fact that the camaraderie is directed toward competition). A group that experiences camaraderie appreciates and respects all of its members, warts and all, and develops strong bonds that come from regularly spending time together. When the time comes to pull together to get work done, the group can draw on the spirit and good will it has developed.

Camaraderie enables a team to unite in the pursuit of ambitious change efforts. Within the work of a reciprocity entrepreneur, it needs to be intentionally cultivated, sustained, and directed. The following section introduces a set of patterns for engagement that enables teams to consciously pursue this kind of camaraderie. These patterns can also structure the way the team engages all other constituencies around the change efforts that they are working on.

From Pattern Following to Pattern Generating

Given the difficulty of reintegrating systems that have been broken apart, the reciprocity entrepreneur needs to have a strong grasp of change theory and how to move large groups toward a shared destiny. One of my mentors, Jim Clark, contributed to a significant body of research undertaken at Harvard University from the 1950s into the 1970s.[1] This study found a set of five critical patterns that were necessary to accomplish permanent individual and collective change. They discovered that these patterns were profoundly effective at pulling people together, even in large-scale endeavors.

1. *Frequency:* Profound change requires, at the minimum, weekly engagement and reinforcement. In other words, you can't wait weeks and months and expect that what had been built in one event will carry to the next. This is one reason why twelve-step programs require people to attend weekly meetings. It also helps to explain why Oprah Winfrey's daily talk show was such a powerful instrument for building a sense of community.

2. *Intensity:* People need to spend a quantifiable amount of time together in order for bonding to take place. This quantity turns out to be 8 to 12 percent of the waking hours within a seven-day period, which translates to one to two hours a day or a full day once a week. There are ways to decrease this quantity, but the original research found that most successfully bonded groups followed one or the other of these two patterns.

3. *Duration:* A group needs to gather consistently over time in order to build trust and fellowship that are strong enough to be easily accessed when called for. The research showed that after three to seven years it was really difficult to break a well-developed bond and that it would take significant disruption to pull even one person out of the community. Oprah once said, concerning her effect on the effort to achieve gender and marriage equality, that she felt that her repeated raising of the issue

for her community over the long duration of her show might be one of her greatest contributions. She was aware of the need for extended duration in order to accomplish deep change.

4. *Mentoring:* The ideal mentor is someone who is a part of the community, not set apart from it—someone who has already been successfully on the road ahead of the others, discovering and transforming the obstacles encountered along the way. The personal stories that this mentor can offer, the empathy that she can genuinely exhibit, and the ability to draw out the same power in others without expecting them to do things the same way she did are important characteristics of this pattern. In other words, the mentor's maturity and personal development are essential for helping a group to overcome its fragmentation and move toward a shared destiny.

5. *Holism:* To become comrades, members of a group need to work on not only skills and ability, but also traits such as character, attitude, and self-directed motivation. A mentor's ability to keep these aspects in harmony is the deciding factor in many groups; simple skills and functionality have little effect on the experience of camaraderie. In the study, mentors would call for reflection and discernment, asking people to assess their own values and how well they were being lived out. They would encourage both reintegration of anything that had been excluded and reflection on the resulting effect on the overall development of community. This work was every bit as important as getting something done.

The experience of camaraderie and the appreciation of diversity are closely linked. Multiple perspectives, diverse windows on life, help us reintegrate the split-off parts of ourselves, enlarging our sense of self and community and strengthening our common work.

Camaraderie with Nature

As a reciprocity entrepreneur grows in her work, she comes to realize that camaraderie need not be limited only to human beings. It can be extended to include all living systems. We can become "brothers and sisters" to the animals we share the planet with, and colleagues to the rivers, forests, and wetlands. When we spend enough time with nature, we can enter into a collaborative relationship that can benefit the whole world.

Regenesis Group, a New Mexico–based design consultancy, calls on this aspect of reciprocity as a core dimension of their work. They are highly skilled at evoking and enabling camaraderie and reciprocity between human communities and natural systems. Through a process called "story of place," Regenesis has the ability to help humans and nature talk to one another. The resulting narrative unifies the birthing and evolution of both human and natural communities and reveals what their destiny could be together. This helps people speak meaningfully of place as alive, and of the distinctive characters or personalities of their own places.

Regenesis helped the planning team for Loreto Bay, Mexico, discover that the new town was sited on an estuary that had been bulldozed and filled in by the Mexican government many years earlier to prepare the way for tourism development. The government had inadvertently shot itself in the foot, because the real draw for tourism was the healthy and diverse marine life in the Sea of Cortez, and the estuary had played a key role in maintaining and contributing to that life. Regenesis worked with the planning team to create a design for the new town that included a network of living canals throughout the community to restore the function of the estuary and reintegrate the residents with the work of nature in that place. The camaraderie that this built came from the inspirational power of the story that residents could tell: their deep care for their place was literally bringing it back to life.

Shadow: Isolation

A Hunter drops into the shadow expression of her archetype when she loses contact with her mission to provide for the larger community. In a disaster situation, for example, a healthy Hunter helps to organize her community to ensure that everyone, regardless of social standing, is fed and cared for. By contrast, the shadow Hunter withdraws into her well-stocked bunker and loads the guns. Both are concerned with provisioning, but in the shadow expression the Hunter has collapsed into a solipsistic and defensive stance. An extreme negative manifestation of isolation is the hoarder, whose pathologically irrational behaviors (like storing up years of old newspapers) are an attempt to defend against an overwhelming world.

These shadow characteristics present a real danger for the reciprocity entrepreneur, who must manage them by becoming constantly mindful about the real meaning of wholeness. Reciprocity entrepreneurs are at their best when they remember that their purpose is to serve their communities by fostering the kind of collaborative leadership that makes it possible for everyone to be invested in the goal of wholeness.

You can see the shadow side of the reciprocity entrepreneur playing out in certain aspects of Oprah's career. Her enterprises carry her name, and, with two exceptions, she is the only person ever to appear on the cover of *O Magazine*. She walks a fine line between branding in order to maintain a platform for her work and falling into the shadow, where the weight of responsibility rests on her shoulders alone.

12

Reciprocity Entrepreneurs
Michiel Bakker and
Annalie Killian

No culture can live if it attempts to be exclusive.
—MAHATMA GANDHI

Reciprocity entrepreneurs are often *intra*preneurs—internal agents who use organizational resources and platforms to do sustained work on large-scale change. Michiel Bakker is a good example of an intrapreneurial change agent.

Michiel Bakker: Shifting Cultural Paradigms and Beliefs

When Bakker joined Google after spending a number of years in the resort industry, he tells me that he felt as if he'd been handed a parachute at ten thousand feet and was expected to jump out of the plane and land on a specific spot on the ground!

Bakker had rapidly worked his way up in the Starwood chain of hotels and resorts, a fairly predictable corporate culture in which he ended up as head of a major division in Europe, the Middle East, and Africa. His first job at Starwood took him from the Netherlands to the southern United States, where he encountered what for him was a startling separation between the highly educated management class and the workers, many of whom were immigrants with limited English language skills. His own cross-cultural upbringing had taught him that language skills are not necessarily indicators of intelligence, capacity to learn, or character. As an operational leader, he designed worker development paths based on the belief that people will work through any barrier if their work culture supports it. This resulted in the promotion of capable people into the management ranks.

In a recalcitrant industry, this shift enabled him to quickly move into general management roles. From there he was able to take on the European portion of the company, where language barriers are more endemic and more complex than in the United States. In some ways, he felt that his international experience with Starwood had prepared him well for the next step in his career, but Google turned out to be another universe entirely.

Pillar 1: Wholeness

When Bakker joined Google, he stepped into a company culture with a long-standing commitment to the health of its employees and their guests. This culture was pervasive and showed up even in the vibrancy of the spaces where food was served. In this context, it didn't take Bakker long to realize that if he was to take Google's intention to heart, he couldn't act as though life began and ended at the threshold to the corporate campus. All Googlers had home lives, and most of them ate food prepared by other people at least part of the time. As Google's director of Global Food Services, Bakker realized that the commitment to healthy employees needed to extend to life off site, through education and programs that would include families and children.

This first wave of innovative programming stimulated a new insight for Bakker and the Global Food team: Google families also operate within food cultures, and more often than not, those cultures encouraged unhealthy behaviors. The team needed to expand their vision to encompass a transformation of global culture and behavior with regard to food. It was a very big idea, but they got to it through knowing that they could not live out their objective of healthy Googlers without it. In this evolution of thinking and mission, Bakker was pretty clearly taking on the role of the reciprocity entrepreneur. He had the capability to move his mind up and down scales of nested systems, from employees to families to communities to large-scale food systems and back again.

Bakker believed that there was a key intervention point (or node) in this global food system that had to do with how the public accesses and integrates information about the connection between health and nutrition. He hypothesized that if he could shift the nature and quality of conversation about this topic, he would not only influence individual behavior but also empower people to influence the world around them. So he set to work gathering a cross-sector consortium of key players to work directly on our image of food and its role in health. Named the Google Innovation Lab for Food Experiences, this group included scientists, media people, educators, civic leaders, food industry leaders, and behavioral experts, bringing together diverse perspectives to create a rich and holistic dialogue about how to create healthier citizenries and food cultures.

The members of the Innovation Lab are all tops in their fields and active leaders in the movement to transform the global food system. By bringing together their diverse perspectives, Bakker aimed to increase their influence through collaboration, shared information, and colearning. Google's role was to provide the platform that would allow this group to assemble the information it needed and disseminate the insights it generated. This vibrant exchange has enabled participants to develop increasingly holistic strategies and launch a host of new projects.

Pillar 2: Significance

Bakker's big shift came when he saw that he was working on nourishment not only for Googlers and their visitors but also for their families, communities, and cultures. Although it was important to feed people well within the walls of Google, he realized that what was really significant was to foster healthy continuity with what lay outside those walls. No more "It's impossible to eat well when I travel."

Bakker could see that this was going to require more than just healthy ingredient substitution and a vegetarian option on every menu. Corner cafés and global companies, grocery stores and farmers, and food providers in every part of the chain of production and distribution were going to need to reorient themselves to the idea that their primary purpose is to generate increased health. In order to make a real change, the food team had to work on what was really significant—generating new cultures that shift what we ask for and collectively expect from the global food system.

Pillar 3: Destiny

The Google Innovation Lab for Food Experiences was established to create dialogue among diverse and knowledgeable participants, with no expectation of achieving agreement across all of the systems represented. Agreement isn't necessary, but without the conversation, cultures will remain ignorant, blind to, and unconscious of the systemic consequences of their food systems. All of the activists participating in the Lab will benefit from an increased capability to develop global imperatives, test them for validity, and use them to guide behavior, even as they upgrade their articulated imperatives over time. These imperatives are like a lighthouse beacon, providing no answers but giving orientation and direction within which better-informed choices can be made.

Bakker came to this work from a lifetime of taking on challenges beyond his existing capabilities. Again and again he has tested himself—changing nations, changing industries, and then working to transform the huge and fundamental food industry. "Humans have unlimited potential to contribute when they are developed and challenged," is the imperative that has guided him along the way.

Yet there is risk in taking on the transformation of something so pervasive. Probably the greatest challenge that Bakker continues to wrestle with is the effect of his vision on the people around him. It becomes so big, so exciting, and so compelling that people become scattered and risk working themselves to death trying to pursue it. Nevertheless, this work has a solid and supportive home within Google, which has developed a culture that expects and encourages a high level of visionary ambition in its managers. Global imperatives, as they are evolved by this group, will continue to provide a sense of direction that increasingly harmonizes the diverse efforts of everyone involved.

Pillar 4: Camaraderie

Before life at Google, when he was still a member of Starwood's management team, Bakker knew that if he was to successfully integrate those who were being excluded for their limited English, he was going to need to involve his colleagues. He insisted that there was no correlation between intelligence and skill in a new language. He introduced the topic into every meeting and decision-making process, so there was no way the problem could be ignored. He did this skillfully, engaging people rather than judging, so they were able to share his perspective. Team after team began to shift, and Bakker's efforts became increasingly visible and valued at higher and higher levels of the organization. The camaraderie that developed within operational teams and the results it produced were communicated up through the hierarchy.

At the Google Innovation Lab for Food Experiences, Bakker used collaborative conversations to build a sense of camaraderie among diverse participants, each of whom represented discrete and fragmented dimensions of the food web. By design, this was very different from the kinds of approach that participants encountered at professional conferences in their field. First of all, he wanted them to see this group not only as a reliable source of learning but also as a resource for making major changes; therefore he was very strategic about who he invited.

Out of their semiannual meetings, participants organized themselves into cross-cultural task forces to implement and carry into their organizations and communities the rich thinking that was emerging. Because people were working together on something of great significance, Bakker was confident that they would develop trust in one another and that they would come to respect and value the widely different perspectives that were brought to the table. He committed Google's resources and creativity to this ambitious change process, knowing that it was consistent with the company's mission to make the information needed to make good decisions readily available.

Shadow: Isolation

Bakker has told me that he often runs the risk of being too far out in his thinking, which can cause him to lose connection with his team members and those directly around him. His challenge is to make sure that all participants come along, cocreating the journey so that it belongs to them collectively. A particularly insidious problem shows up when people start to rely solely on his thought process and initiative because they assume, reasonably enough, that he's going to figure it out anyway. If this goes on too long, the work becomes his and not theirs. This creates isolation for him and robs team members of their own agency and creativity, seriously undermining their esprit de corps.

Bakker makes a real effort to work collaboratively rather than take on all the responsibility himself. He has had to learn to strike the right balance between inspiring and leading on the one hand and engaging the contribution of his colleagues on the other. He has found that sometimes something as simple as stating that a change was made as the result of the input of one of them keeps the team advancing together. Another strategy he has developed is to offer his thoughts only after everyone else has spoken.

Annalie Killian: Paradigm Change in Post-Apartheid South Africa

Annalie Killian shares with Michiel Bakker the outlook of the Hunter archetype, as well as a history of successfully filling her entrepreneurial role from within very large organizations. Killian was hired in 1989 by BHP Billiton to introduce quality circles (a Japanese-invented management approach) to aluminum smelter operations. She was mindful of the political milieu in South Africa, which was undergoing intense change during the lead-up to the release of Nelson Mandela from prison. She was acutely aware of the aspirations of the employees she was working with;

most of them were black and had endured a long history of exploitation in the work place.

Killian quickly encountered distrust and sabotage from shop stewards and trade unions, who feared that productivity improvement would threaten jobs. She recognized this as a valid concern, and worked to shift the conversation to one of developing black employees into leaders capable of running successful companies in the future. At that time, there was not a single black employee in the leadership ranks of the company. Through her unfaltering commitment to the development of these employees, Killian earned their trust, and the quality circles leaders gained recognition and skills that led many of them to become the first South African blacks ever to be promoted to first-line supervisors and leaders.

This early success enabled Killian to convince Billiton Aluminum, part of the global BHP Billiton Group, to allow her to shift focus from productivity improvement at the plant level to capacity building at the community level. The company was in the middle of building the largest greenfield aluminum smelter in the world and had constructed a work camp for the thirty-five thousand laborers needed on the project. Killian saw a major opportunity for the company to anticipate and prepare for the end of apartheid, and she convinced management to completely rethink how to use this camp and its facilities at the end of the project as an engine for community development.

The camp was extensive and made up of large buildings—dormitories, mess halls, storage warehouses, and staging areas for construction. The plan had been to tear it down and sell it for scrap once smelter construction was completed. Killian proposed that it instead be repurposed as a community college campus and small business incubator. Her ambition was to help grow the economic, education, and self-governance skills of the black population so that it could flourish in the new South Africa, thereby ensuring a peaceful and prosperous transition for all.

This purpose informed everything that followed. Once the aluminum smelter project was built, members of the local community were given extensive training in repurposing the dormitory buildings as schools, and they earned construction worker qualification in the process. A host of nonprofits were attracted to the community college campus to collaborate on rebuilding the education system for local children, with a focus on experiential learning and a twelve-year education development intervention, for which Killian's group won the Nelson Mandela Award for Education in 2000.

The high-profile nature of the project attracted participation from a "United Nations of NGOs" working throughout Zululand, many of whom eventually established permanent offices in the NGO Office Park on the campus. Ultimately, the management of the campus was turned over to a locally established nonprofit governing entity that has continued to manage it as a community resource and has rented out space on site to a wide variety of NGOs and businesses to ensure its long-term viability.

Annalie Killian's next big venture took her to Sydney, where she joined AMP, one of the oldest and largest financial services companies in Australia. Her brief was to shake up its 160-year-old business culture and bring more innovation into its operations. Her first impulse was to expose people to new ideas and thinking by taking them outside the business to conferences, workshops, and lectures—but nobody signed up! That's when she realized that she would need to bring the new thinking inside and get in the way of their comfort zones. She came up with the idea of a pop-up university, and she named it "Amplify."

Initially she got people's attention by setting up exhibits and working prototypes of innovative ideas, organized like obstacle courses right in the AMP offices so that no one could avoid getting caught up in them. People liked it. Then she pulled together top experts from around the world to speak on disruptive trends, emerging technologies, and changes in consumer behavior and values. She challenged her speakers to make their specialized topics interesting and relevant to a lay audience of actuaries, accountants, business decision makers, and investment advisors. This, too, was a hit.

These programs became more frequent and extended, and Amplify became established as a learning festival. Employees began to promote the speakers that they had found particularly inspiring to one another, their customers, and their contractors. An invitation to attend Amplify became one of Sydney's hottest tickets. As a result, AMP became what Killian calls "creatively restless." Employees regularly self-organized into groups to explore the significance of new information brought in by speakers, in terms of both their own work and how they could better serve clients, and the company's ability to be a good corporate and global citizen. This led AMP to research a host of new fields, and it has transformed the way companies throughout Australia and beyond think about how corporations learn.

From these stories, one can see Annalie Killian's characteristic way of working on *wholeness*. In South Africa, she helped BHP Billiton see itself as working on a new nation that was trying to come into existence. In the process, the company confronted and helped transform the unconscious patterns that had disenfranchised the majority of South Africans. Every activity needed to build a new plant became an opportunity to simultaneously build a new nation.

Killian then took what she had learned to Australia, where she helped AMP's people break out of their entrenched financial paradigm to see that they were part of a large, complex, interesting world that they had mostly been ignoring. By instead embracing and learning from that larger world, they could not only serve their customers better but also make increasingly positive, reciprocal contributions to their communities, nation, and planet. There was no end to what they could learn and create.

For BHP Billiton's black South African workers, *significance* came not only from becoming self-determining but also from contributing to the future viability of their communities. The idea of being set free through education and skills to build a better life for themselves and their neighbors was highly motivating at this historical moment. Killian anticipated and focused on the capabilities that they were going to need to accomplish this as she worked with community members to rebuild their educational infrastructure.

For AMP, significance came from a change in the way it conducted business. From being product and service oriented, the company embraced the idea that customers should be empowered through their financial decisions. A concrete example is Killian's current project, which

explores customer aspirations for meaning and purpose beyond accumu-
lating savings for their retirement years. The company is figuring out how
to help them transition into a third and deeply enriching phase of life
centered around entrepreneurship, volunteering, and giving back. Killian
envisions AMP as the ideal midwife to a movement that provides support, planning, and connections to enable retirees to successfully launch
the next phase of an engaged and meaningful life.

As a native South African, Killian knew that for her country to
pursue its *destiny*, "Equity needed to become universal." By persuad-
ing BHP Billiton to turn its vast construction camp over to local people
as a force for community development, she laid out a direct path for
Zululand's people to own the vision and the means for creating their
future. Supported by ongoing education, this direct control over their
own destiny through their first community foundation finally gave people
in Zululand a real voice in how their community was developed.

At AMP, Killian recognized that the primary human destiny of
"creative restlessness" was being thwarted by a bureaucratic hierarchical
culture. With the Amplify festival she democratized learning and opportunity, inventing a means by which people's certainties could be dislodged
and new leaders, insight, and innovation could emerge.

Killian has learned that *camaraderie* has to be grown through sustained effort and meaningful interaction within a shared commitment.
She immediately saw that converting the BHP Billiton construction
camp into a vibrant campus would enable diverse nonprofits, educational
groups, business start-ups, foundations, and government agencies to create the scale, duration, frequency, and intensity of contact that would
foster pulling together for a common vision that went far beyond tribal
or racial divides. This has allowed the project to successfully outlive her
own involvement and even the active participation of her company.

In Australia, Killian's experimentation enabled her to establish a
similar rhythm of frequency, duration, and intensity at the Amplify fes-
tivals. She varied the size and scale of events and expanded the festival to
the point that it is now held monthly and is open to customers, partners,
and the public. Out of this environment of lively exchange have arisen

diverse cross-functional teams working on new products and ventures that have nourished AMP as a partner in innovation and a global leader in open learning systems.

Shadow: Hanging On

With regard to the shadow of this archetype, Annalie Killian reports that she has to pay attention to her tendency to hang on to things. She gets so attached to the whole of what needs to happen that it becomes a struggle for her to relax her control over execution. This can cause her to isolate herself from the team or community she is trying to serve, a particularly difficult issue when it comes time to pass responsibility on to the next generation of leadership. She fears that without her things will fall apart and the carefully woven whole will lose its integrity. To manage this fear, she keeps telling and retelling her team the story of what their project is all about, so that everyone is holding and contributing to the same vision. She reminds herself that it takes a community to bring about significant change, and that she alone could never do it.

Build Your Roadmap: Ideas for Shifting Cultural Beliefs

Promote understanding of the whole and wholes within wholes.

Make it real. Demonstrate what wholeness on a grand scale actually looks like.

Determine what is significant and base your work on it.

Articulate the global imperatives that will call stakeholders together around a common purpose and destiny.

Make your work visible so that others can learn to see what you see.

Build camaraderie that will endure long after you are gone.

Impact Investors: Visit www.ResponsibleTrep.com/downloads to download your free workbook to apply *The Responsible Entrepreneur* concepts to investing your funds, guiding owners in making a difference, and evolving the investment industry.

13

Revitalizing Founding Agreements
Four Pillars of the Regenerative Entrepreneur

Justice must always question itself, just as society can exist only by means of the work it does on itself and on its institutions.
—MICHEL FOUCAULT

Wilma Mankiller was the first woman to be elected chief of the Cherokee Nation. She was speaking as a Headwoman when she had this to say about how native peoples have survived European contact: "We are constantly revitalizing tribes. After every major upheaval, we have been able to gather together as a people and rebuild a community and a government. Cherokee people possess an extraordinary ability to continue moving forward, because our culture, though certainly diminished, has sustained us since time immemorial. We find our way back to it and forward from it."[1]

Headmen and Headwomen work on transforming our relationships—as businesses, communities, and nations—to the founding documents, ideas, and agreements that bring us together and unite us. They are interested in the core purpose of governance, which is to provide the structure, stability, and opportunity to enable a people to express its true potential. Time and again, they direct their people's attention to the deeper meanings behind the organizing principles of the institutions to which they belong in order to offer a new experience of what these institutions are really for and what they have the potential to be.

In addition, the Headman has played the role of the visionary who awakens vision in others. He knows that he serves all of Life—past, present, and future—and that he serves best when he enables all beings to serve, according to their own natures.

As a Headman, a regenerative entrepreneur revitalizes his community through images and stories that remind people of their lineage, their origin, and the times when they have all stood together. This helps people remember what really matters and who they really are. It reminds them that they are unique, with something unique to offer. The regenerative entrepreneur is concerned with essence at every level of the system, and with keeping the experience of essence alive for people through time.

Regenerative Entrepreneurs Unify Us Around Uplifting Purposes and Principles

The chief pursuit of the regenerative entrepreneur is unity. Businesses, groups, or nations are made up of individuals. It takes a high order of leadership to unify them around an uplifting purpose and set of principles. In the Western world, and particularly in the United States, there is a tradition of individualism that, when carried to an extreme, devolves into anarchy or an inability to create order. In a disunited community, diverse abilities and perspectives have no way to be reconciled toward some larger purpose. The work of the regenerative entrepreneur is to reveal unifying purposes and principles that inspire the desire to be a part of something larger, to work for its success, and to support its evolution.

The Four Pillars of the Regenerative Entrepreneur

The four pillars of the regenerative entrepreneur orient her to the potential embedded in the essence of every living system, including living institutions created by human beings (see Figure 13.1). These bind people together in order to achieve collective purposes of a higher order than any individual could accomplish alone. Businesses, universities, cities, and national governments are all examples.

Pillar 1: Transformation

Transformation is the overarching goal of a regenerative entrepreneur. Transformation literally means to enable something to go beyond its current form in a way that is irreversible. Once you bake a cake, you can't unmix the ingredients. For the regenerative entrepreneur this change of form is always intended to enable an entity to generate more value than it could in its prior form. Most of the life and work of a living entity is carried out through transactions with its environment. In the flow or process of those transactions, there are relatively few points at which a transformation can actually occur. In the case of a cake, for example, these show up when you mix the batter and when you put it in the oven. At

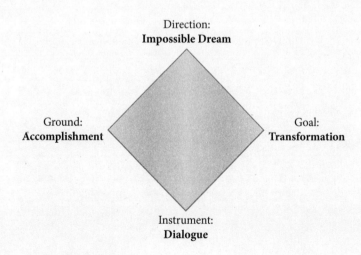

Figure 13.1   Regenerative Tetrad

those points, the change in form becomes irreversible and something new has been brought into existence. The challenge for a regenerative entrepreneur is to look at something as complex and unmanageable as a nation and locate the key points at which beneficial transformation can occur.

Undertakings of such scale and ambition require discipline and rigor and, almost inevitably, some method for making the complexity of systems intelligible and manageable. This is the core purpose of systemic frameworks such as the ones introduced in this book (see Figure 13.2). A particularly useful framework for thinking about large-scale system transformation is a hierarchy of eight goals, organized around the key points at which any complex system can be transformed. A regenerative entrepreneur holds all of these goals and their relationships in mind, although in a given moment or context he may choose to emphasize only one of them. This kind of work is challenging but doable, and you can see it reflected in the thinking, rhetoric, and choices of great nation builders.

- *Cohesion—where wholes become unified:* The regenerative entrepreneur builds unity and cohesion. When something is cohesive, it's difficult to pull apart. It may flex and adapt, but its integrity is maintained. It can withstand external forces and even be strengthened by them. Without cohesion in society, it's hard to maintain order and function. Everyday life

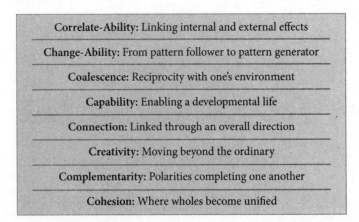

Correlate-Ability: Linking internal and external effects

Change-Ability: From pattern follower to pattern generator

Coalescence: Reciprocity with one's environment

Capability: Enabling a developmental life

Connection: Linked through an overall direction

Creativity: Moving beyond the ordinary

Complementarity: Polarities completing one another

Cohesion: Where wholes become unified

Figure 13.2   Hierarchy of Goals

becomes difficult when we don't feel like we're all in it together. It's also difficult to elevate society, to make it better, when we don't agree on what we're unified around. When you have cohesion, you get a multiplier effect because all of the energy is going in the same direction. All parties have their shoulder to the same wheel, pushing together. For example, community cohesion often increases after a natural disaster or in preparation for a shared celebration.

- *Complementarity—polarities completing one another:* The regenerative entrepreneur takes that which seems divided, unrelated, contradictory, or oppositional and reframes it as that which is necessary for wholeness. People often experience the world dualistically—right and wrong, good and bad, insider and outsider, true and false—and they are clear about which side they accept and which they repudiate. The regenerative entrepreneur is able to stand above and outside of this dualistic experience and help others see how the two sides are actually two halves of a whole. This is what the yin-yang symbol represents: two opposites nested in each other, each containing a part of the other.

- *Creativity—moving beyond the ordinary:* The regenerative entrepreneur enables individuals and groups to believe in themselves as people with agency, which frees them to see possibilities that had previously not been apparent. He is not so much a source of creative ideas as an illuminator of the process that brings people together to lift themselves into an exciting future. When a group can do this, its members become originators and owners of their ideas, which is very different from having been given someone else's creative idea to work on.

- *Connection—linked through an overall direction:* For a community to be healthy and viable, all members need to exercise their individual creativity in ways that move the whole forward. The most effective way to do this, and therefore a goal of the regenerative entrepreneur, is to help people feel connected to an overall direction. This enables them to see how what they are working on at any point should intersect with the work of others toward this direction. When people are connected through a shared direction, they can assess when it is necessary to communicate with one another and what is most meaningful to communicate. This allows them to work independently without losing touch with the experience and purpose of collaboration. In *Good to Great*, Jim Collins introduced the idea of "hedgehog concepts," in which a goal is both meaningful and big enough that everyone is going to need to pull together to achieve it.

- *Capability—enabling a developmental life:* The regenerative entrepreneur starts from the premise that all people are inherently capable of growth. He supports the ability of people to work on themselves and thereby to contribute more to the collective. One of his methods is to invite people into roles that are beyond their current capability. He affirms his belief in them and works with them to develop themselves. This is more than acquiring new skills and knowledge; it requires learning to self-manage and self-motivate. This work increases each person's access to her own competence. The regenerative entrepreneur doesn't undertake this process as a supervisor, assigning new work. Rather, he engages individuals to help them discover roles that will advance their capability, while at the same time assessing the appropriate fit of those roles within the overall direction of the company. This creates a thriving culture in which people willingly pursue tougher and tougher challenges.

- *Coalescence—reciprocity with one's environment:* Growth and nourishment depend on an exchange with our environment and are sustainable only when that exchange is reciprocally beneficial. The regenerative entrepreneur seeks to join and bond with—coalesce with—the growth and success of her stakeholders. Instead of seeing stakeholders as people to get something from (an extractive mindset), the regenerative entrepreneur strives to enable stakeholders to realize more of their potential (a value-adding mindset). The exciting part of this shift is the momentum that gets built as each party is enriched by the exchange and therefore able to contribute more through time.

- *Change-ability—from pattern follower to pattern generator:* Let's face it, human beings get into ruts. This is a tendency we share with other great apes, all of whom project into the future what they've learned from the past. Humans have the additional and very powerful capacity to image a different and better future and to move themselves and their communities toward it.

This is why one of the primary roles of the regenerative entrepreneur is to engage people in *imaging* patterns of living that promote viability and vitality for all stakeholders. (Imaging is different from visioning, which is almost always rooted in past experience.) This experience has a unifying effect. It makes change less divisive or frightening. It makes change inspiring. A powerful enough image can bypass the tendency to resistance and fear, and can produce the motivation to overcome the restraining energies that keep us stuck. But images are fragile and need to be regenerated periodically.

The regenerative entrepreneur helps people break out of their ruts by realigning them to an image of what is possible so that they can generate new patterns of behavior. Many businesses move managers around regularly as a way to develop their capacity to adapt, make sense of unfamiliar patterns, and land on their feet. A more sophisticated approach that produces fewer side effects is requiring people to take on large-scale challenges for which there are no precedents—a practice that Google has applied very successfully.

• *Correlate-ability—linking internal and external effects:* Regenerative entrepreneurs see strong correlations between their internal states (and the states of their businesses) and the external effects they are able to create in the world. For this reason, they know that they must maintain a continuous practice of personal development. They also invite others to make this correlation, because they know how critical it is to grow appreciation for reflective thinking within their company's culture. This is especially challenging for Western business leaders, because reflection is not part of our education and is not highly valued in the go-go world of corporate success. A reflective culture can be developed, and it will have a business payoff, but it takes time and commitment.

Pillar 2: Accomplishment

Accomplishment has a special meaning for a regenerative entrepreneur. In general, an accomplishment is some capability we have developed within ourselves, such as singing an aria or baking a perfect soufflé. But for a regenerative entrepreneur, it has more to do with discerning the right indicators that a system is evolving in a beneficial direction.

From a traditional business perspective, accomplishment is something that you work to develop personally, in your team, and for your organization as a whole. But for a regenerative entrepreneur, the real purpose of business is to enable the accomplishment of his downstream customers and other stakeholders. For example, rather than measuring his own yields or waste, he measures the increase in his customers' success with regard to yields or waste.

Measuring Success from a Value-Adding View. If you envision a flow of materials from earth to earth—through your supplier's hands, through your operation, though your customers' consumption or conversion— you have a better idea of how the regenerative entrepreneur invites people to manage and measure accomplishment. How well do your customers serve their communities and buyers, and how can you help them do better? How about your other stakeholders? Are the communities you impact becoming better able to provide for the wellbeing of their members? Are the ecosystems you affect getting healthier? Are your suppliers creating increasingly valuable inputs to your business and becoming more economically viable in the process?

Accomplishment comes from making the difference others are counting on you to make. I call this a value-adding view of life because its focus is on helping everyone you interact with become better able to add their value. This is the value you bring to them. One company I know invited its customers and suppliers to participate in its annual strategic planning sessions. The guests would report on their future plans and desired performance improvements, and then everyone would get into small groups to figure out how to make them happen. Sounds fun, doesn't it?

Pillar 3: Impossible Dream

In "The Impossible Dream," the hit song from the musical *Man of La Mancha*, Don Quixote sings of his aspiration to "follow that star, no matter how hopeless, no matter how far, to fight for the right without question or pause, to be willing to march into hell for a heavenly cause."

The big question for the regenerative entrepreneur is, "What does it mean to fight for the right?" Not surprisingly, a regenerative answer goes beyond conventional ideas of right.

Often what is right is framed in a fairly concrete way. Businesses talk about it in the context of tasks: "Do it right, preferably the first time." A more sophisticated thought is "Work on the right thing," which recognizes that one can do a task perfectly and yet be working on something that may not matter in the long term. Philosopher Matthew Fox made the concept more developmental when he called on businesses to "Do right work." This thought challenges individuals and organizations to bring their decisions into integrity with their values, taking into account the many other people and systems they affect.

Regenerative entrepreneurs hold themselves to a higher standard, one based on the understanding that all entities affected by a business are evolving toward their own uniqueness. The challenge for them is to "Do what's right for all through doing what's right for each." This is very different from trying to do one thing that is right for everybody, and as an idea that is alien to most business decision making, it is a sort of impossible dream. Yet just as with so many impossible dreams, if you are willing to follow that star, what started out as impossible can change the world.

Google has been working with indigenous peoples in the Amazon. It is developing devices that allow them to use Google maps to communicate the actual effects of logging on any given hectare to the government, logging and oil companies, and the public. This has created a more level playing field for native communities, who in the past have been outgunned when it comes to access to technology and information. Now they are able to bring real-time data into the conversation. Google believes that this makes decision making more transparent and more inclusive. Already they see shifts in how industrial interests interact with native communities.

Pillar 4: Dialogue

The regenerative entrepreneur works on change through skillful engagement rather than top-down directives or simplistic participatory processes. What distinguishes a regenerative level of work is developmental dialogue.

Developmental dialogue starts from the premise that no one knows the answers to the most important questions. They must be discovered or revealed through the engagement itself. This promotes intellectual curiosity, self-awareness, and, at its best, deep caring about the outcome. Genuine dialogue destabilizes our certainties and allows something new to enter our thinking.

The purpose of developmental dialogue is to awaken capacity for new insight and wisdom. It isn't training, which seeks to transfer knowledge and skills from an expert to an initiate. Rather, it is the act of tapping expertise, of which everyone has some, in order to do something creative. By extension, dialogue isn't about finding the answer that someone in the room already knows. Rather, it is about discovering answers that no one has had before.

Dialogue is also different from voting or polling, which assume that the average is the answer. Developmental dialogue evokes ideas that did not exist when the engagement began and enables people to evolve their opinions and positions. It is not a debate, in which one side seeks to convince the other with the weight of evidence or passion. Nor is it a social conversation, in which one person endeavors to unconditionally appreciate and understand another without any concern for goal or outcome. A developmental dialogue has the express intention of advancing a group along a path that is collectively invented and leaving no one behind.

To foster developmental dialogue, a regenerative entrepreneur needs a set of advanced capabilities, all of which are learned with time and dedication:

1. Prevent oneself from being mechanical (that is, from automatically repeating old mental patterns).
2. Develop the ability to act as midwife to the birth of new ideas and direction in others.
3. Understand and work on pattern rather than just responding to form.

4. Work with every person with humility, as if there is no difference in class or level.
5. Recognize that the work is never finished; understanding is never complete; and the search should remain open ended and alive.

Some regenerative entrepreneurs have a rare gift for fostering this kind of dialogue on a national or international scale. For example, Larry Page has regenerated our understanding of what information is and who should have access to it, and of what investment is and who should be able to participate in it. Using Google as a platform, he has been able to turn institutional inertia against itself, so that the rules society operates by are suddenly questioned and reframed.

Shadow: Aloofness

Regenerative entrepreneurs are able to see and seize opportunities for fundamental change because of the depth and consistency of the inner development they engage in. But that can become very heady work.

All the regenerative entrepreneurs I have known have struggled against the tendency to build distance between themselves and their troops, colleagues, and customers. They see so much at once, and not all of it can be explained in a few sentences. They sometimes see the land mines along the way to their goals, and they try to find a clear path. To avoid worrying everyone, they carry this knowledge alone. As a result they can seem aloof, hard to approach, and sometimes hard to understand.

Most regenerative entrepreneurs are aware of this shortfall and work on it. They structure events to allow people to ask them anything they want. They sit in on team meetings. They agree to interviews and to having their thoughts published. But it is not easy. The long view they hold and the complex paths they need to pursue make regenerative entrepreneurship an inherently lonely and hard-to-understand role to fill.

14

Regenerative Entrepreneurs
Jay Coen Gilbert and Shainoor Khoja

The impossible often has a kind of integrity which the merely
improbable lacks.
—Douglas Adams

Regenerative entrepreneurs have the habit of redefining what we think
is possible. They have the visionary capacity to see their ideas as if they
had already been realized, so much so that they will speak in present or
past tense about something no one has ever seen. They move back and
forth in time in their mental experience, and this can be confusing to
people around them. They don't do many interviews, because the world
they see is so different from the world that exists that they can become
impatient with explanations.

Jay Coen Gilbert: Evolving the Idea of Incorporation

Like Larry Page, Jay Coen Gilbert exhibits many of the qualities and characteristics of a regenerative entrepreneur. But he came to it differently; he

saw the course of his life change suddenly and irrevocably during a tragic two-week period that began with the 9/11 terrorist attacks. Already devastated by shock when the twin towers fell, Gilbert lost his father to cancer a week later, and then a business partner in a car accident a week after that. He describes the experience as having a hole torn in his reality. In the grief that followed, he entered a period of deep questioning that led him to recognize that he wanted and needed to completely change the direction of his life.

Already a successful entrepreneur by the time he was in his late twenties, Gilbert decided to act swiftly and wholeheartedly to embrace a commitment to social justice and ecological health, values that he had always kept in the background. He had the clear sense that he needed to do everything in his power to transform the way humans care for one another and for Earth.

He joined forces with two college friends, Andrew Kassoy and Bart Houlahan, to establish B Lab. Their big idea was to redefine success in business based on their insight that government and the nonprofit sectors were necessary, yet insufficient for the task of addressing the world's most challenging problems. The power of business was needed not only for the creation of individual wealth but also for the creation of healthy communities. Business needed to be seen as a tool for enabling humans to realize their full potential, by providing livelihoods that served as ways to contribute to the whole. B Lab set out to make it easier to integrate higher purpose into the workplace and to recognize and reward people for their contributions to achieving it.

The B Lab team knew that they would have to challenge and redefine the body of regulations and laws that force corporations to make all decisions solely on the basis of shareholder value, preventing them from taking into account the broader social and environmental implications of their actions. Since its inception, B Lab has pursued this vision by means of three interrelated strategies designed to support competition among businesses to be the best in the world at being the best *for* the world.

Gilbert describes their first strategy as a certification that makes it easier for people to support good companies, not just good products or marketing campaigns. B Corp certification functions in the marketplace like fair trade or organic certification, but it addresses a whole company, not just a cup of coffee or carton of milk. Although an LEED certified green building was a good thing, what difference did it really make if the people who worked in the building were treated poorly and harmful waste was being dumped out the back? Certification at the level of the B Corp enables customers to judge a company by the whole of its impact on all of its stakeholders. Since 2007, B Lab has certified more than nine hundred B Corps from more than sixty industries in thirty countries. (A number of the companies mentioned in this book are B Corps, including Seventh Generation, Indigenous Designs, Fishpeople, and Roshan.)

The second strategy is development (state by state in the United States, to start) of a body of law, regulation, and precedent for accepting and validating this alterative corporate structure. In the United States, and seemingly in most jurisdictions around the world, corporations are required by law to serve one purpose: maximize return to shareholders. This means that, no matter how regenerative the perspective of company leadership, every action must be justified by how it helps the company become more profitable. If one's primary reason to be in business is to serve society, then this conception of the purpose of business is limiting.

To create more freedom for member businesses, Gilbert and his partners worked with corporate attorneys from across the country to draft model legislation for a new corporate structure, a legal entity called a benefit corporation (B Corp for short). Organizing as a B Corp gives legal protection to management and directors to consider the impact of their decisions on society, not just on shareholders. Importantly, this protection runs two ways; investors in a B Corp also have the legal tools to hold management accountable to achieve their stated social purpose. This gives entrepreneurs a new way to build scalable, purpose-driven businesses, while aligning interests with a growing community of impact investors who want to find and support businesses that can make them money *and* make a difference.

B Lab's third strategy is the creation and promotion of cost-free assessment and analytical tools that give any company or investor the means to measure, compare, and improve their social and environmental performance. The B Impact Assessment is already used by more than sixteen thousand businesses around the world as a framework and road-map to serve the good of their workers, communities, and environment. B Analytics is a customizable data platform for investors to benchmark and report on the performance of their portfolio companies with regard to social and ecological as well as financial equity. It is used by UBS, USAID, and scores of other large private and public investors with billions of dollars in assets.

As Gilbert has pointed out to me, these three strategies, taken together, have the effect of moving all the key players—businesses, policy makers, and investors—forward in a coherent way toward a new conceptualization of the roles of business and capital in society. They have carved out and built a structure around a small but growing niche in the global economy that enables business and capital to be put to work in service of the common good. This is exactly the kind of influence that a regenerative entrepreneur seeks to have in the world.

To those standing outside the work of Gilbert and his partners, the work of the regenerative entrepreneur may seem difficult to visualize; indeed, almost beyond imagination. This is the power of the Headman archetype, which taps into possibilities that have never before been manifested. What gave Gilbert the strength to assume this role went beyond his experience as a successful entrepreneur. It also came from the efficacy of his impossible dream, his creative partnership with Kassoy and Houlahan, B Lab's innovative strategies, and a willingness to take risks, make mistakes, and allow ideas to unfold over time.

Pillar 1: Transformation

Looking at the B Lab through the lens of the hierarchy of eight goals for system transformation, one can see Gilbert working on all eight simultaneously.

1. At the level of *cohesion*, B Lab created B Corp, a fully conceived and unifying concept that allowed people to see what a responsible corporation could look like as a whole.

2. At the level of *complementarity*, this new B Corp had the effect of revealing the weaknesses in the existing models of corporate structure and pointing to how they could be addressed.

3. At the level of *creativity*, B Lab created a template that gave all kinds of businesses the specific benchmarks and criteria that would enable them to evolve themselves and measure their own progress.

4. At the level of *connection*, B Lab created a branded presence in the minds of consumers that allowed businesses that were meeting a high standard of integrity and verified performance to be certified by a third party.

5. At the level of *capability*, B Lab enabled investors to accurately assess and report on the social and environmental impact of investments, thereby attracting previously sidelined capital to socially and ecologically beneficial enterprises.

6. At the level of *coalescence*, B Lab broadly published and promoted its methods, so that over time they have been widely adopted, not only by businesses but also by nonprofits, community activists, and even governments.

7. At the level of *change-ability*, B Lab went state by state (including to all-important Delaware, where more than half of all American companies and nearly two-thirds of the Fortune 500 are incorporated) to promote the adoption of the B Corp as an acceptable legal model for a business—leading eventually, many hope, to its designation as a tax-preferred entity.

8. At the level of *correlation*, B Lab has worked diligently to shift from the association of business with corruption to an association with benefit (hence the name *B* Corp).

Pillar 2: Accomplishment

Gilbert has evolved what gets measured with regard to business and capital markets in a way that reveals the systemic implications and impacts of business activities. B Lab gave businesses a way to measure whether they were evolving a whole, rather than breaking out and addressing individual issues (such as fair trade or carbon footprint). They were specifically trying to defragment corporate approaches to responsibility.

First, their assessment methodology shifted emphasis off of the list of activities that a company was engaged in and onto the actual effect the company was having in the communities it impacted. Second, it placed responsibility squarely on the board of directors, who were expected to assess and to take responsibility for the company's behavior as a whole.

Pillar 3: Impossible Dream

From the beginning, B Lab's impossible dream was "harnessing the power of private enterprise to create public benefit." Early on, Gilbert and his partners had a significant opportunity to clarify for themselves what this could mean. They had been invited by a California legislator to present model legislation that would make it permissible for business to consider nonfinancial interests when they make decisions, which was not allowable in California at that time.

The legislation was passed and sent to Governor Arnold Schwarzenegger, a pro-environment Republican. Instead of signing it, as everyone expected, he vetoed and sent it back with a note explaining his decision (a rare occurrence indeed!). The note encouraged the legislature to explore the creation of an entirely new corporate form to address this need—a far more effective approach than monkeying around with existing corporate statutes.

Gilbert reports, "We left with our tail between our legs, but that veto led to the formation of a legal working group that drafted the legislation to create a new corporate entity that came to be called the benefit corporation or B Corp. It took literally five years to the day from that veto to inclusion of the B Corp into Delaware's approach to corporate structure."

Pillar 4: Dialogue

Finally, B Lab is demonstrating that transforming engagement from debate to dialogue is the most effective way to create change at this level. One of the most powerful dialogues currently emerging is the one between publicly traded companies and the privately held B Corps that they are acquiring. As B Corps have matured, they have become candidates for acquisition by larger publicly traded companies with potentially very different philosophies and almost universally different legal restrictions. (So far, the B Corp phenomenon has been limited, for the most part, to privately held companies where there is less likelihood of legal challenge from shareholders. This is more complicated for private B Corps with outside venture or private equity investors, but even for these, the parties know each other directly and choose each other intentionally, and the B Corp legal structure and transparency requirements help align interests and create mutual accountability.)

In these negotiations, B Lab has taken an active role in preparing B Corps to successfully transition from a defensive stance, whereby they attempt to ensure the ongoing integrity of their mission, to a proactive stance, whereby they seek to influence the mission of the larger parent company. They accomplish this through educating their B Corps in how to use the buying process as the beginning of an open and ongoing dialogue that will help to evolve both companies. The B Corp becomes the agent of change for its new parent, introducing a new set of criteria and values that allows the larger company to step onto a more demanding and compelling platform of corporate responsibility.

Shadow: When I asked Gilbert to describe his own shadow and how he worked to embrace and manage it, he gave me a list that included words like *curt, dismissive, distracted, unavailable, intimidating*, and *unapproachable*. He asked his colleague Stephanie Ryan to offer her perspective. She said that she sees his shadow showing up when he visits member organizations. She joked that you can't shut him up. He has so much capacity to speak to the issues and the opportunities connected to the B Corps idea that listeners can feel like they are drinking from a fire hose—and she can't move the agenda along. But she also observed that she can see him working to stay present and accessible all the time. Gilbert ended by saying that what really matters is how people perceive him, causing Ryan to add that "lack of reflection" was definitely not part of his shadow.

Shainoor Khoja: Rebuilding a War-Torn Nation

When Shainoor Khoja arrived in Kabul, Afghanistan, in the fall of 2003, she found a city devastated by war. She had come to start a business that could help rebuild a country—an *impossible dream* that she had pursued for years. She had already developed practical skills in Pakistan, Poland, and parts of Africa, but Afghanistan was where she turned those skills toward nation building.

In 2003, infrastructure for utilities, transportation, and communications was virtually nonexistent, let alone services like health care and education. This made it impossible to create enough economic growth to generate the tax revenues needed to rebuild. Even if money had been brought in from outside the country, there weren't enough business skills to put it to use and jumpstart the economy. Through the long years of war, the Afghan population had become dependent on the limited services provided by national and tribal governments, and the private sector had all but disappeared. Many had written off Afghanistan as a lost cause. But a lost cause was exactly what Khoja was looking for, and fortunately she was part of a volunteer community that shared her mission.

In partnership with private funders who had a strong desire to make a fundamental difference in some of the world's most intractable trouble spots, Khoja was in Afghanistan to look for proactive ways to help a traumatized population come together as a nation. To do this, she and her funders believed that it would be necessary to rebuild faith in the possibility of nationhood and self-governance. They were seeking a means to make this real for the Afghan people as a practical matter in their daily lives.

After a few false starts, Khoja and her husband were able to organize a team with the shared commitment to using business as a means for healing a nation. They believed that the core issue facing the Afghan people was the absence of opportunities to exercise self-determination. After generations of serving as a proxy battleground, first for the Cold

War and then for the war on terrorism, ordinary Afghanis found themselves struggling to survive in a dangerously shifting political climate. Khoja and her colleagues came to recognize that the reestablishment of self-governance would require building the kind of basic infrastructure that allows people to take charge of their lives in ways large and small. This is why they decided to focus initially on telecommunications, which offered a kind of scaffolding from which other infrastructure could be developed.

This thought represented a real breakthrough for Khoja, whose background up to that point was in health care. Her original plan had been to set up health clinics, but she soon realized that this approach only served to reinforce an attitude of passivity in the population. She didn't want to introduce yet another aid organization trying to patch up the damage. Instead, she reasoned, an infrastructure-generating business could provide open-ended opportunities for people from all walks of life who wished to pursue their own aspirations using their own creative capacity. AKFED, a private fund of the Aga Khan Foundation, provided the initial capital to establish Roshan Telecommunications and build an extensive network of cell towers.

Since then, Roshan has grown into the largest nonmilitary employer in Afghanistan. It sells phones and services to consumers, as well as infrastructure access to other providers. The company's business model is based on establishing small, locally owned franchises in communities throughout the country and then using the presence of these businesses to foster self-reliance and community redevelopment. In the absence of a functioning government, this has been critical to getting Afghani communities back on their feet.

By responding to the intense and pent-up need for a communications network, the business immediately secured its viability. It then leveraged this position by using the purchase and consumption of cell minutes as a perfect opportunity to teach ordinary people basic financial skills. Bear in mind that 75 percent of the population was living on less than two dollars a day at that point and had no way to improve their situation. This education in basic financial skills was the first exposure most of them had ever had to the concept of banking.

Roshan has continued to focus on building financial and business capability, enabling local people to grow into a wide range of roles within the business. For example, the company decided that one of its earliest ventures would be mobile access to banking (including microloans). Given that there was so little financial capability in the country, this seemed like a leveraged way to make an enduring difference. Roshan invested extensive hours and large sums of money to train officers who could judge the investment-worthiness of projects. This represented a major learning and growth opportunity for these officers, who were set on a path of becoming well-paid professionals.

In every community where it does business, Roshan provides development services, including education, health clinics, and playing fields for children. The idea of a local business sponsoring local activities, while commonplace in the United States, was completely new in Afghanistan, where for generations government had provided everything. Little by little, communities where Roshan had a presence began to connect the dots. Local residents could see that the phone services they were purchasing from local owners were generating a stream of revenue that was flowing back into the community in the form of social benefits. The economic activity of ordinary people was creating a virtuous cycle of community development. This awakening to the possibility of being able to shape one's own destiny—for individuals as well as for communities—was the *transformation* that the company wanted to bring into existence.

Shainoor Khoja aimed to grow a culture where, little by little, ordinary people believed that they could take control of their lives. At the time of this writing, Afghanistan still suffers the effects of prolonged war, but Roshan is providing an experience of a different kind of narrative of *accomplishment*. Ordinary individuals can do something about conditions in their communities, and they can begin to trust and work with one another toward common purposes. Personal agency became the indicator that Khoja's group adopted as a basis for its decisions. Ready access to communications technology has been the means by which it has worked to generate this shift, along with the local franchise model, which bases economic development on personal relationships among neighbors.

Given Afghanistan's long history of ethnic conflicts, Roshan has been exceptionally sophisticated and successful at gently initiating *dialogue* among previously antagonistic groups. For example, the sports fields it has built are explicitly open for all, a message underscored by the fact that there are no fences around them. Roshan has also established schools to serve both boys and girls wherever it has a business location. Because poverty is so high, schools are free and in session for half a day, and they provide a free midday meal to encourage children to attend. The company also offers health care to everyone connected with it, a service that had hitherto been available only tribe by tribe, and one to which women had no access. Within Roshan, everyone has been treated equally, rather than as competitors for scarce health care services.

Shadow: With regard to shadow, Khoja reports that when she originally had the idea of using telecoms to provide basic health services, education services, and farming services, "It was difficult for some of the management team to get this, and I was so passionate that I would take the risk and push them into initial acceptance at times. Once the concept became a reality, they could see it and then would get behind it. Sometimes that push appeared as though I thought I knew better, and I personally could sense that, but I was determined and did truly believe it was possible."

Khoja is fortunate to have a spiritual practice that helps her rein in her runaway ideas. Also, Roshan's nonhierarchical governing structure has provided an environment of open conversation and dialogue that helps her stay connected.

Build Your Roadmap: Ideas for Shifting Cultural Beliefs

Identify the key points where a truly beneficial transformation can occur—the work to be done at the pivot point in order to produce:

- Correlate-ability: Linking internal and external effects
- Change-ability: From pattern follower to pattern generator
- Coalescence: Reciprocity with one's environment
- Capability: Enabling a developmental life
- Connection: Linked through an overall direction
- Creativity: Moving beyond the ordinary
- Complementarity: Polarities completing one another
- Cohesion: Where wholes become unified

Define new measures of accomplishment based on the success of the whole.

Establish dialogue groups and reflect on the set of advanced capabilities and how to increase them in the group.

Impact Investors: Visit www.ResponsibleTrep.com/downloads to download your free workbook to apply *The Responsible Entrepreneur* concepts to investing your funds, guiding owners in making a difference, and evolving the investment industry.

Part Four

The Game of Changing the Game: Using Domains, Archetypes, and Communities of Practice to Foster Change

I think it matters whether someone has a good heart.
—ELON MUSK

This book opened with the founding of the nation of Botswana through enlightened collaboration among all four leadership archetypes. I want to close it with the story of one entrepreneur, Pamela Mang, and her company, Regenesis Group. Mang and her colleagues have learned to move fluidly through all of the archetypes in order to influence all four domains.

I offer you a challenge, a call to action. Are you ready and able to step up to the role of responsible entrepreneur? Or have you been in such a role for years and are now ready to make a bigger promise? Are you drawn to engage in the disciplined practice described in these pages, so that your business and your investments can cause the changes you want to see in the world? Then I invite you to join the growing community of intensely creative people who are defining the game of business for the twenty-first century.

Listen to interviews of Responsible Entrepreneurs who are *changing the world:* www.ResponsibleTrep.com/bookbonus.

15

The System of Archetypes at Work
Pamela Mang and Regenesis as an Instrument of Change

The major problems of the world are the result of the difference between the way nature works and the way people think.
—GREGORY BATESON

Pamela Mang, my friend and frequent ally, demonstrates the qualities of a woman called to be a responsible entrepreneur. She continuously works on developing her thinking and her state of being in order to serve as an agent for the transformation of increasingly complex systems. As a regenerative entrepreneur, she is also the cofounder of Regenesis Group, a company explicitly dedicated to regenerating the way human beings develop and inhabit ecosystems. Her story is interesting because it shows how all four levels of archetype can be integrated into a single business venture.

Even as a young woman, Mang was called to work on change at the national and global scale. After completing her studies at Stanford in the 1960s, she and her husband helped create an organization that brought together China scholars, journalists, and politicians to open a new era of dialogue between the United States and the People's Republic of China. This effort laid the foundation for bringing the PRC into the United Nations.

It was during this early career in political organizing that Mang first developed the core insight that has guided everything that followed. She was working as a field secretary for the American Friends Service Committee in San Diego County (at the time a very conservative part of the country) on minority economic development, social justice, and peace. She had teamed up with a local minister to organize the area's first march against the Vietnam War. She was determined to bring together the diverse groups working on the issue because she recognized that the progressive community was too small and fragmented to have an impact if it didn't form a coalition.

Although she was able to get these groups to meet and agree that a march was necessary, the whole project fell apart over the question of what kind of signs would be allowed. People let their ideological differences get in the way of the larger shared purpose. For Mang, this was a vivid demonstration of the fact that until people can manage themselves, they will never be able to make the larger changes they aspire to. Enduring change, she intuited, needed to start from an internal shift in human consciousness. This integration of inner development with outer change efforts has become a signature of her approach in all her subsequent ventures.

After she lost a child to bone cancer, Mang entered a period of deep introspection and questioning about how to use her life in the most meaningful way. This led her to set up Communication Advocates, a venture to help nonprofits do a better job engaging communities of support. She found that no matter how good her community development strategies were, the internal dysfunctions of the organizations she was serving would undermine them from the get-go. Once again, internal development was the key missing ingredient.

Find a Teaching and a Teacher

Mang began to investigate organizational development, which eventually led her to the work of Charles Krone, the pioneering systems thinker who also mentored me. In Krone's work she finally encountered a body of theory and practice that successfully integrated inner and outer development. She spent a number of years applying Krone's theories, assisting teams that were leading change processes at large multinational corporations. Her hypothesis was that changing the consciousness of individuals could lead to change in these highly influential organizations and could shift their impact on human potential and the health of the planet.

Years after the fact, she reported that a casual interaction with Krone had a profound and lasting impact on her. He said in passing that it was his belief that regeneration is the work of the twenty-first century. This struck a chord in her. The question, she realized, was not whether to work on regeneration, but how and where. While serving on the board of the World Business Academy, she met a group of people who believed that human beings are an integral part of nature and that the key to restoring the health of the planet was to restore humans to consciousness of their proper role in the biosphere. This, she realized, was where she needed to be working—on the regeneration of the relationship between human beings and planet Earth.

Found a Business to Change a World

Not long after, she and her husband, Robert Mang, cofounded Regenesis as a way to test the premise that there were two fundamental requirements for moving people to take responsibility for their relationship with nature: first, they have to experience the kind of connection that causes them to care about it, and second, they need to understand how nature works in order to exercise that care intelligently. The mission of Regenesis is to awaken people to their role as sources of a healthy planet by developing their caring about and understanding of the places where they live and work, so that the way they develop and manage those ecosystems can be transformed.

From the beginning, Mang recognized that this mission would require working in all four domains and therefore through all four archetypes. Toward this end, she set out to foster an organizational culture that integrates the internal development of team members with the external development of strategic projects. The team she assembled immediately resonated with this idea. They had all spent years trying to shift the way human beings develop and interact with ecological systems but had not had the kind of broad impact they aspired to. In a sense, they already represented the four archetypal perspectives. Mang's task was to help them draw out and develop their capacity to move forward collectively as an entrepreneurial organization dedicated to changing a very big game. She firmly believed that the real power of this organization would show up when all involved became responsible entrepreneurs together.

Regenesis Works in All Four Domains

Regenesis always starts from its intention to work on regeneration, on transforming the systems and structures that limit the full expression of human and ecosystem potential. This is a very different starting place from, for example, energy rating systems or certification programs for building materials. It was clear from the outset that governing policies and infrastructures strictly limit what's possible in the arena of land use, locking in development standards and procedures that produce a host of unintended negative consequences.

Founding Agreements

Rather than work directly to change these policies, Mang and the Regenesis team looked at why communities create philosophies and policies of land use in the first place. Land use policy, they observed, usually comes from a desire to protect the integrity, character, and resources of a community. Behind the regulations and prohibitions lies a deep (and sometimes unconscious) caring for place. They asked themselves: What would happen if communities could engage proactively in strengthening and increasing that core character of place, rather than fighting rearguard actions to keep it from being destroyed? This led the company to invent a methodology called "Story of Place," which captures in narrative form the distinctive qualities and dynamics that make a place unique and suggests ways to integrate that uniqueness into planning, policy, and economic development.

In the border town of McAllen, Texas, a thriving center for international trade, Regenesis was invited to contribute to an interaction between the city and a development team, who were working together to regenerate a section of the inner city. By introducing Story of Place, Mang and her colleagues helped the group see that the city's identity and economic strength had always depended on flow and exchange—along the Rio Grande, across the Mexican-American border, and among diverse constituencies. The development team conceptualized a new central park for the city, where the whole community would be able to connect with one another as well as with the water, wildlife, and many visitors flowing through. This represented a significant change from what had been previously proposed: a fairly conventional downtown retail and entertainment complex with expensive apartments and amenities for a high-end market. The result was embraced by the community, and it helped influence how the city thought about a host of other economic and development issues.

Cultural Paradigms

Regenesis also works on *reciprocity*, bringing about greater wholeness in individuals and cultures by exposing and transforming their paradigms or belief systems. Implicit in the Story of Place is a subtle but profound shift in the paradigm governing the relationship between humans and nature. For Mang and her colleagues, human beings are embedded in nature and, like other species, they have a critical role to play in the life, health, and future of the planet. By telling stories of place that show the seamless connection between natural and human systems, Regenesis offers people a way to see this new paradigm in action, within their own lives and experience. From this direct, close-to-home experience, the Regenesis team believes that a culture of reciprocity between humans and nature can be grown.

St. Mary's County, in southern Maryland, had been embroiled for years in conflicts among environmentalists, developers, farmers, fishermen, and various other local residents. At stake was the health and future of the St. Mary's River, which empties directly into the Chesapeake Bay and had been increasingly threatened by development practices and pressures. Each of these constituencies was arguing for their piece of the pie, but no one was advocating for the whole that holds those pieces together. Mang teamed up with local stakeholders to work on changing the belief systems that were driving these conflicts. Together they created stories that brought the entire watershed to life as a living system. Instead of seeing themselves as competing interests, the various stakeholder groups could see themselves as members of a family of living beings, all embedded within the regional ecosystem. Out of this breakthrough insight, they formed a watershed alliance to foster the health of the river on which they all depended and to find creative and systemic solutions for how to live as a community in harmony with its living landscape.

Social Systems

Regenesis works on *reconnection*, seeing patterns and revealing the gaps in collective understanding regarding the impacts of existing social systems. Given her background in organizational development, Mang was readily able to see opportunities for evolving fresh approaches to the public engagement processes that are a standard part of land development and policy debate. Too often, she observed, public meetings devolved into battlegrounds, with the loudest voices and strongest egos carrying the day. She thought it should be possible to use these public processes differently, as a way to help communities generate new realization and connection to conscience with regard to who they were, what they could aspire to be, and how they could bring their social systems into alignment with their unique character. She and the other members of Regenesis began designing and testing approaches that could evoke a more collective sense of identity and purpose from communities.

The Finger Lakes region of upstate New York was mandated by the state to create an integrated sustainability and economic development plan that could demonstrably reduce carbon emissions while producing multiple social and ecological benefits. It decided to adopt the Story of Place approach with the help of Regenesis. Building off of a host of existing initiatives and plans, the team used its understanding of the unique patterns of the region to shed new light on what this collection of overlapping jurisdictions and communities could collectively pursue. This formed the basis for a broad and highly energized public engagement process, in which diverse stakeholders worked together to integrate and upgrade the region's sustainability efforts and to evolve the systems that would support these efforts.

For example, one group wanted to bring together local economic development, ecological management of land and water, CO_2 reduction, and distributed energy production. They also saw the need for improved local resilience in the face of power, communication, and transportation interruptions brought on by increasingly intense storms. They developed a concept for translating the region's high volume of agricultural and dairy waste into a source of renewable energy. They then proposed small-scale, affordable systems that could be used on individual farms or clusters of farms as a way to avoid the environmental and economic costs of trucking heavy materials to a centralized facility. Farms with these local energy systems could serve as sanctuary zones for vulnerable rural populations during emergencies. The group's aim was to produce and test a package system in the region that could be sold in agricultural areas throughout the country. This is highly consistent with one of the region's underlying patterns, which is to take new inventions and useful ideas and democratize them, making them broadly accessible.

Industries

Finally, Regenesis works on *realization*, the creative pursuit of its vision of an improved reality and a better world through transforming how the development industry thinks about itself. Originally the company worked on helping developers exceed community expectations and regulations. By setting far higher standards for themselves with regard to environmental improvement and social contribution, developers had the opportunity to shift their public image from bad guys to community leaders. Regenesis set out to educate and influence diverse partners—from architects to owners, regulators to investors, engineers to builders—about what was possible and how it could be accomplished. Its methodology has evolved over many projects and has generated growing interest in the design and development field.

In recent years, Mang and her colleagues recognized that working one project at a time was too slow and didn't give potential practitioners the underlying conceptual frameworks they would need in order to apply the Regenesis approach for themselves. The team began developing educational programs and a school to enable the professional practice of Regenerative Development to spread around the world.

Use Archetypes to Anchor Great Aims

For Mang, archetypes enable people to get firmly anchored in a particular nature of being and then to look at how this shifts the way they work in the world. Over the years she has dedicated herself to creating this capacity within Regenesis, so that all of its members, collectively and individually, can engage with all four archetypes. She believes that this is important for two reasons:

- Within the company this capacity has provided the kind of learning environment that is critical to promoting lasting and meaningful change, an environment in which inner and outer development are pursued simultaneously.
- All four levels of the change process need to be moved forward at the same time, as they are mutually influencing and reinforcing.

In Mang's experience, the effort to shift foundational agreements is reinforced by work on cultural paradigms, social systems, and industries. When a company holds the idea of regeneration at its core, it's only natural that it wants to translate this idea into projects and methodologies that will influence all of the other levels. As a result of this natural progression, Regenesis has begun to affect multiple arenas, from the development industry up to how entire regions govern themselves.

16

Time to Walk Your Talk
See the Void. Answer the Call. Join the Movement.

None of us want to be in calm waters all our lives.
—JANE AUSTEN

I meet many admirable people who are creating useful products, doing good work in the world, being good role models. Some aspire to be "net positive," so that their businesses create more good than harm, and I am heartened by their energy, creativity, and good conscience. But these businesses, as important as they are, are primarily focused on being exemplary in themselves. In terms of the serious global challenges that humans currently face, I believe that these businesses have aims that are too small, incremental, or unleveraged to achieve rapid systemic change. The world also needs businesses and entrepreneurs with the aspiration to transform fundamental systems.

The four leadership archetypes provide larger-than-life support for the pursuit of really big aspirations. Although we human beings are not ourselves archetypes, we can learn to tap into archetypal energies to help realize our potential. This work is not esoteric, and it doesn't require rare talent; what it requires is practice. You begin where you are, whether you are seventeen or seventy, whether you are an experienced entrepreneur or fresh out of school.

Prerequisite 1: Magnetic Pull

There is, however, a critical prerequisite: you must experience a powerful magnetic pull to face the human condition and the condition of the world and know that you must do something about it. This can be uncomfortable, but it can also have an enlivening effect as you recognize the contribution that is uniquely yours to make. You don't need to be a person who has solved all of your psychological or spiritual dilemmas. You needn't be nice, or fabulous looking, or kind to stray animals. You only need to be willing to keep developing yourself so that the work can be done.

The frameworks in this book are intended to help you respond to that magnetic pull in a leveraged or strategic way. Instead of identifying some small piece of the problem and working on it (a completely honorable thing to do, by the way), an archetypally informed approach to entrepreneurialism applies the same amount of energy to leveraging a node in a system with the potential for global influence.

Prerequisite 2: You Have No Other Choice

How do you know that responsible entrepreneurship is your calling? Well, what I've observed is that you'll know it's a calling when you really *don't* want to do it. In other words, when something keeps showing up in your thinking or in your world that demands that you take action, and you recognize that you really don't know how to do it but it's yours to do, and you keep pushing it away because it's so annoying—*that's* a calling. A true calling is both humbling and scary, because it always demands that we become larger than we believe we can be. But we pursue this kind of work without humility. At the same time, there is an experience of inner necessity that prompts us to accept our limitations and do it anyway, because it must be done, and if we don't do it, maybe no one else will.

Challenges are built into a calling. Here are three significant challenges that I believe are central to the calling of the responsible entrepreneur:

1. *You have to see your business as an instrument, not an end in itself.* "Changing the world" quickly becomes a platitude if you don't know how to go about doing it. You need to figure out where to work on a system to get it to shift and how to use your business to make the shift happen. This means enlarging your definition of business success to include system transformation.

2. *You have to recognize the kind of person you will need to become and commit to the dogged work required.* The archetypes laid out in this book can be particularly useful for this purpose. They provide patterns that you can explore and grow into, patterns that have been discovered, deepened, and imbued with meaning over many generations. Adopting an archetypal role enables you to engage in self-improvement and development with a sense of direction and purpose. It focuses your attention on who you choose to become rather than on who you've been.

3. *You have to rigorously and continuously develop your thinking to manage increasing levels of complexity.* To be able to work on something complex, most people need order. This is why so many people make lists or sort information into categories as ways to manage chaos. Lists and categories are simple frameworks that can be useful for managing what is already known. They are less useful for stimulating creativity or discovering new potential. The responsible entrepreneur tetrads are examples of frameworks designed to develop the thinking needed to work with change and complexity. They support your ability to discern where and how to place your attention strategically in order to accomplish large-scale transformation.

Prerequisite 3: The Right Domain and Archetype for the Desired Change

Each level of domain and archetype represents a different order of change or effect. It is easier to shift an industry than a social system, easier to shift a social system than a cultural paradigm, and easier to shift a paradigm than a foundational agreement. As you move up the hierarchy, the changes become more universal, enduring, and pervasive. The levels of commitment, character, and capability increase correspondingly. There's something exciting and meaningful about progressing toward ever higher orders of calling.

Industry Level

At the industry level you are using your business to change other businesses, so it's fairly direct and focused. You begin by demonstrating that you can be successful within the industry through fundamental changes that you are making in your operations. You then seek explicitly to influence the industry as a whole, so that it begins to adopt the improved way of operating that you have developed. The advantage of working on an industry is that you have a kind of captive audience because everyone is competing within a given market. If you are able to pioneer an evolutionary approach that works, others will follow you—or risk being left behind.

Social Systems Level

At the level of social systems you are using your business to change consumer or citizen behaviors and consciousness. Unlike an industry, which tends to self-organize through professional associations or conferences, the members of a social system tend to be more diffuse and harder to reach. An entrepreneur seeking to transform social systems focuses on key transactions rather than on operations, because this is where the users of your product or service have the greatest level of participation in your business. They are, in a sense, fully present and therefore available for a moment of awakening or learning. Your task is to figure out how to move the transaction beyond a simple exchange to an experience of how their choices affect the larger systems that they live in and care about. This means introducing personal connection and emotional significance into the transaction, as when Fishpeople connects buyers to the captain of the fishing ship from which their dinner came and to the quality of the water in which the fish was caught. It generates a call to conscience and invites people to restore congruity between their deepest values and their choices or actions.

Cultural Paradigm Level

At the level of cultural paradigm you are using business to provide a plausible alternative to deeply held but destructive beliefs (such as sexism or racism). This is work that requires patience and broad reach. Think of the years, the thousands of interviews, and the resources that Oprah has amassed to slowly advance the idea that all people of every color, gender, and orientation are human beings and worthy of respect.

An entrepreneur who is seeking to shift culture to be more inclusive or holistic focuses on the mental processes by which we prove to ourselves, over and over again, that what we believe is actually what is true. Cultural paradigms exist because they are continually reinforced. Your work as a reciprocity entrepreneur is to provide a different story—a different experience—which, when repeated enough, will cause people to recognize that what they thought was true is not. The movement to secure the civil rights of LGBTQ people has succeeded largely because it knew that the belief that alternative sexual identities were evil and monstrous would crumble when people discovered that their friends, colleagues, and family members were gay.

Not surprisingly, people who want to pursue this level of work are generally attracted to industries and businesses where sustained public engagement is possible (such as media, education, or certain kinds of retailing). If you aspire to be an agent of profound cultural change, you must become skilled at touching people's hearts rather than changing their minds, because mind changing is something they must be invited to do for themselves. This is why reciprocity entrepreneurs are not advocates and are very careful not to be perceived as taking sides. Their credibility and their influence comes from the ability to embrace all sides, portraying the stakeholders involved through stories and actions as members of the same human and planetary family.

Founding Agreements Level

Change at the level of foundational agreements is the most difficult kind of change to accomplish. It requires you to use governing infrastructure—such as legal precedents, corporate charters, or governmental institutions—to accomplish its own evolution. Your focus here is on the intention behind the laws and institutions we create to govern ourselves and on how to manifest those intentions in a more perfect and beneficial way. Businesses interact with governing bodies in a myriad of ways: everything from paying taxes to meeting standards of safety or professionalism.

A regenerative entrepreneur seeks to upgrade those interactions so that governance and government become agents of health and continuous improvement, rather than barriers to creativity and aspiration. To do this, you must go back to the original spirit of the policy or law or institution or nation, and reconnect people to its life and meaning so that it can have new purpose as it moves into the future. You must then put this regenerated interpretation into action so that people experience how it is consistent with the original intention while standing in stark contrast to the interpretations that preceded it.

Prerequisite 4: Your "Change the World" Roadmap

I want this book to enable you to take the idea of changing the world and put it into action in a powerful way. I've provided what I believe can serve as a guiding pattern for moving from an inspiring (although abstract) concept to concretely manifesting what you care deeply about.

I've introduced three elements of this guiding pattern. The first is a hierarchy of domains within which change can occur. This provides a framework for locating the nature of change you wish to pursue.

The second is a corresponding hierarchy of archetypes and roles that depict the nature of character you must build and exhibit in yourself to have a transformational effect on your chosen domain. Each role is accompanied by a set of four pillars that describe the means it uses to accomplish its corresponding level of change.

The third are the stories themselves, which present ordinary people doing extraordinary things. Stories help us remember what we are trying to achieve, and they help us project ourselves into the pattern of thinking and response that we need to learn if we wish to also make change that is extraordinary.

The key to getting started is finding or convening a community of people who, like you, are pushing themselves to affect a larger arena. All of the people whose stories I told in this book were embarrassed that I had singled them out, because every one of them recognized their indebtedness to a group of colleagues and co-thinkers. By community, I don't mean a group of people working under one roof. I mean people who come together intentionally to evolve their thinking in a disciplined and reflective way. When human beings come together to challenge and assist one another in living up to this kind of aspiration, there is no reason why they can't turn the world onto the healthier course that is so urgently needed. This is why I am hopeful.

Where do you stand with regard to *your* call?

Listen to interviews of Responsible Entrepreneurs who are *changing the world:* www.ResponsibleTrep.com/bookbonus.

Notes

Introduction

1. "How the Great Recession Spurred Entrepreneurship: In Weak Local Economies, Startup Numbers Are Strong," strategy+business, June 21, 2013 (accessed January 29, 2014), http://www.strategy-business.com/article /re00240?pg=all.
2. Sandip Sekhon, "Crowd Funding Statistics and Trends [infographic]," GoGetFunding, May 1, 2013 (accessed January 29, 2014), http://blog.goget funding.com/crowdfunding-statistics-and-trends-infographic/.

Chapter 3

1. Walter Isaacson, *Steve Jobs* (Kindle edition) (New York: Simon & Schuster, 2011), location 517.

Chapter 4

1. Richard Branson, *Losing My Virginity: How I Survived, Had Fun, and Made a Fortune Doing Business My Way* (New York: Crown Business, 2007), p. 535. Except as noted, all other quotations in this chapter are from this source.

Chapter 6

1. Carol Sanford, *The Responsible Business: Reimagining Sustainability and Success* (San Francisco: Jossey-Bass, 2011), pp. 245–259.

2. "Larry Page: 'Google Should Be Like a Family,'" *Fortune* at CNNMoney (money.cnn.com), January 19, 2012 (accessed January 29, 2014), http://tech .fortune.cnn.com/2012/01/19/best-companies-google-larry-page/.

3. Chris Gaylord, "Maria Montessori and 10 Famous Graduates from Her Schools," *Christian Science Monitor*, August 31, 2012 (accessed January 29, 2014), http://www.csmonitor.com/Innovation/Tech-Culture/2012/0831 /Maria-Montessori-and-10-famous-graduates-from-her-schools/Google -founders-Larry-Page-and-Sergey-Brin.

Chapter 7

1. Clayton M. Christensen and Hal Gregersen, "The Secret to Keeping Your Company Alive," Inc., April 16, 2012 (accessed January 29, 2014), http:// www.inc.com/clayton-christensen/how-to-keep-company-innovative.html.

2. Douglas R. Conant, "How to Influence People Like a CEO," Conant Leadership, n.d., http://conantleadership.com/influence-people-like-ceo/.

Chapter 9

1. Richard H. Thaler, director of the Center for Decision Research at the University of Chicago Graduate School of Business, interviewed fifty-five scientists who gave him examples of this phenomenon as it has appeared throughout history and shared research findings on why it occurs. Many examples are online at http://www.edge.org/3rd_culture/thaler10/thaler10 _index.html. Thaler is also coauthor of *Nudge: Improving Decisions About Health, Wealth, and Happiness* (New York: Penguin, 2009).

2. Roland Gribben, "I've Been a Tax Exile for Seven Years, Says Branson: Virgin Chief Confesses Love Affair with His Caribbean Home," *Telegraph*, October 13, 2013 (accessed January 29, 2014), http://www.telegraph.co.uk/finance /businessclub/10376341/Ive-been-a-tax-exile-for-seven-years-says-Branson .html.

Chapter 11

1. The Harvard studies were overseen by Professors Fritz Roethlisberger and Elton Mayo, and by James V. Clark, who was then a research assistant and later a professor. They were the natural outgrowth of research in industrial management begun in the 1930s by a team at Western Electric, which resulted in the first real understanding of social intervention in industrial change. The behaviors it focused on were alcoholism, smoking, regular exercise, delinquency and recidivism in criminal activity, language learning, and immigrant socialization. Researchers looked at individuals

working independently and at those working in collective programs to support change (such as Alcoholics Anonymous). Parts of the Harvard studies appeared in many publications, but because Professor Roethlisberger died before he authorized closure and final publication, they were never brought together as a whole. James Clark, who worked with both professors throughout the entire project, provided much of the reporting on outcomes and implications. He also headed the board of directors of the Community Chest (later called United Way) for several years and helped many non-profit change organizations, such as Alcoholics Anonymous, benefit from the study. I was a protégé of Professor Clark for twenty-five years, and he was a member of my doctoral committee. The world is forever indebted to him for the guidance he provided to effective change efforts based on his forty years of research and practice.

Chapter 13

1. "Wilma Mankiller Former Principal Chief of the Cherokee Nation." Powersource Gallery, http://www.powersource.com/gallery/people/wilma .html.

Acknowledgments

My deepest gratitude goes to those who worked up close and deeply to make this book readable and elegant. First is Ben Haggard, my long-time writing collaborator. He is a creative being to his core and takes precious time from his art and community collaborations with Regenesis to make my ideas sing. I would not be an author without him. Kit Brewer and Shannon Murphy are also collaborative creators on wording and the arc of the book. They add harmony and excitement through their rigor in presentation.

Jossey-Bass team: thanks first to my developmental editor, Jenny Ng, whose suggested restructure led to a better design for layout and idea flow. Brilliant! To Karen Murphy, who kept me on track and on brand message. To Kathe Sweeney, who first believed in me, and Jesse Wiley, who took me on and taught me the publishing business. And to Drew Banks, who connected me with them all.

To my friends, colleagues, and clients who agreed to be in this book as stories that teach: they are people I love and admire; I have been blessed to be in their lives. They exposed their amazing lives and businesses, including their shadows. They were hidden treasures, now revealed.

About the Author

Carol Sanford is founder and CEO of The Responsible Entrepreneur Institute and Essence Alignment Co., a global consultancy. She has worked with clients such as DuPont, Procter & Gamble, Intel, Agilent, and Seventh Generation, and has taught as a lecturer on business, urban planning, and entrepreneurship at many universities, including the MIT Sloan School of Management, Stephen M. Ross School of Business at the University of Michigan, and Rotman School of Business at University of Toronto. Carol is a regular keynote speaker at global conferences. She blogs for the *Economist, CNBC, CSRWire, Stanford Social Innovation Review,* and other outlets, and her award-winning first book, *The Responsible Business* (Jossey-Bass, 2011), is used as a text at Harvard and Stanford and at the Google Innovation Lab for Global Food Experience.

Carol currently lives in Seattle. For more information, please visit www.theresponsibleentrepreneurinstitute.com or www.carolsanford.com.

Index

Page references followed by *fig* indicate an illustrated figure.